Signs of Agni Yoga
HIERARCHY

HIERARCHY

1931

Agni Yoga Society
319 West 107th Street
New York NY 10025
www.agniyoga.org

© 1933, 1977 by the Agni Yoga Society.
First edition published 1933. Third edition 1977.
Reprinted 2017. Updated July 2020.
Translated from Russian by the Agni Yoga Society.

ISBN: 978-1-946742-82-7
ISBN (eBook): 978-1-946742-12-4

Merging into the waves of the Infinite, we may be compared to flowers torn away by a storm. How shall we find ourselves transfigured in the ocean of the Infinite?

It would be unwise to send out a boat without a rudder. But the Pilot is predestined and the creation of the heart will not be precipitated into the abyss. Like milestones on a luminous path, the Brothers of Humanity, ever alert, are standing on guard, ready to lead the traveler into the chain of ascent.

Hierarchy is not coercion, it is the law of the Universe. It is not a threat, but the call of the heart and a fiery admonition directing toward the General Good.

Thus let us cognize the Hierarchy of Light.

How to transmute the most bitter into the most sweet? Naught save Hierarchy will transform life into a higher consciousness.

It is impossible to imagine a bridge into the Infinite, because a bridge is in need of abutments. But Hierarchy, like the abutments of a bridge, brings one to the shore of Light. And imagine the entire effulgence that the eyes behold! And understand the Song of Light.

Let us labor for Light and Hierarchy!

HIERARCHY

1. So much has been said about doctrines; yet humanity does not know how to accept the doctrine of the Brotherhood. How many distortions have been accumulated about the Truth! How many principles have been destroyed! They will ask, "On what is the Stronghold of the Brotherhood built?" Answer, "On the doctrine of the heart, the doctrine of labor, the doctrine of beauty, the doctrine of evolution, the doctrine of tension—the most vital doctrine."

We are Votaries of the Infinite. Where the all-encompassing striving cannot penetrate, the Brothers of Humanity do not affirm their manifestation. We suffuse space with the flux of evolution. The Brothers of Humanity willingly renounce Paranirvana for the affirmation of human evolution, in their desire to lay the foundation for a better step. The goal is not divested of labor. The goal is not divested of sacrifice. Thus, point out the closeness of the manifestation of Maitreya.

According to the prophecy of the most ancient Teachers, when humanity loses the foundation of the Teaching and sinks into obscurity, the Epoch of Maitreya will take place.

Our pillars of the foundation are sent to regenerate the spirit-understanding. Thus say to those who do not understand, thus point out the doctrine of the Heart!

2. When We pointed out the urgency of regenerating Our Decrees concerning the equilibrium of the Origins, humanity did not accept this assertion and

inaugurated transgression. Thus, one side transgressed against the cosmic balance.

We know the tread of the Mother of the World. We know the manifestation of the Mother of the World. We intensify the complete flow of the Magnet to restore the doctrine of the Heart.

I designate the Tara as the symbol of the assertion of Our Decree. Yes, yes, yes! The Tara and the Arhat bring to humanity a Covenant of utmost striving. Thus is the future built. Thus We affirm Our striving. Wondrous is the future!

3. The heart of an Arhat is like the Heart of Cosmos. The heart of an Arhat is like the fire of the sun. Eternity and the motion of Cosmos fill the heart of the Arhat. Maitreya is coming, radiant with all fires. His Heart is aflame with compassion for destitute humanity. His Heart is aflame with the affirmation of the new Covenants.

Among people there exists the concept of benumbed Arhats; and poor yogis feed the imaginations of men with their own images. But when humanity shall realize that the Arhat is the highest manifestation of Materia Lucida, it will understand that there is no difference between Materia Lucida which emits Light, and the Matter of Love enveloping all with Light. Humanity invests the Arhat with an austere image, but Materia Lucida radiates Love.

The sublime is bestowed upon the sublime; and the sublime dwells in the sublime; and the sublime will hold sway in the dimensions of the far-off worlds.

4. Our Hierarchy lives and grows by the fiery law. We Arhats rejoice at the fire of life, and even more at the growth of the flame of evolution. Future Arhats, completing their earthly accounts on the planet, are co-workers with Us, the Arhats. When Hierarchy is enriched, there is a cosmic festival. The law is one and eternal. The law is confirmed by Cosmos.

We see the radiance of the worlds. We see the accomplished and endless march. We see the radiance of the Mother of the World! Let us conclude in the joy of the endless march.

5. The universal Eye of Shambhala brings Bliss to mankind. The universal Eye of Shambhala is a Light on the path of mankind. The universal Eye of Shambhala is that Star which has guided all seekers.

For some, Shambhala is the Truth. For others, Shambhala is a utopia. For some the Ruler of Shambhala is a venerable sage. For others, the Ruler of Shambhala is the manifestation of riches. For some, the Ruler of Shambhala is a bedecked idol. For others, the Ruler of Shambhala is the Ruler of all Planetary Spirits. But We shall say, The Ruler of Shambhala is the fiery Impeller of Life and of the Fire of the Mother of the World. His Breath is ablaze with flame and His Heart is aglow with the fire of the Silvery Lotus.

The Ruler of Shambhala lives and breathes in the Heart of the Sun. The Ruler of Shambhala is the Invoker and the Invoked. The Ruler of Shambhala is the Sender of the Arrow and the Receiver of all arrows. The Ruler of Shambhala breathes the Truth and affirms the Truth. The Ruler of Shambhala is invincible, turning destruction into construction. The Ruler of Shambhala is the Crest of the Banner and the Summit of Life. Accept the Ruler of Shambhala as the manifestation of life; thrice I say—of life! For Shambhala is the guaranty of human aspirations. Our manifestation is guaranty of the perfecting of humanity. Our manifestation is the affirmed path to the Infinite.

6. All creation is contained in the call of the heart. The entire cosmic expanse is permeated with a call, and the Heart of Cosmos and the heart of an Arhat are permeated with the call. The call and the answer comprise the combination of the cosmic fires. Union is verily the manifestation of our cycle. Many cycles are created by the call, and these, expanding intensely, embrace different spheres. The affirmation of creation is manifested as union.

I, Ruler of Shambhala, say, "The principle of life is the affirmation of the expanse of cosmic energy and the way of creative Fire!"

7. The Ruler of Shambhala reveals three Doctrines to humanity: the Teaching manifested by Maitreya summons the human spirit to Our creative world; the Teaching of Maitreya ordains the infinite in Cosmos, in life, and in the attainments of the spirit; the Teaching of Maitreya guards the knowledge of the Cosmic Fire as the unfoldment of the heart that embraces the manifestation of the Universe.

The ancient legend that affirms the manifestation of Maitreya as a resurrection of the spirit is correct. We will add that the resurrection of the spirit as the conscious acceptance of the Teaching of Lord Maitreya may be precursor of the Advent. Verily, the resurrection!

8. Maitreya wishes to hasten all. Maitreya wishes that all should be successfully accomplished. Maitreya wishes you joy. Maitreya wishes to grant to humanity a gift through the fiery experience of Agni Yoga. Maitreya wishes to transform life on Earth in the radiance of the Mother of the World. Yes, yes, yes! The beauty of life is limitless!

An Arhat sees with the eyes of the heart. An Arhat sees with the eyes of the heart the beauty of reality. An Arhat sees with the eyes of the heart, and the essence of the future calls Us. Verily is that creativeness affirmed by Us.

9. Ruleress, I pronounce Thee the great Co-worker of Cosmic Reason. Ruleress, thou, beyond all cosmic powers, bearest within thyself the sacred seed which provides radiant life. Ruleress, affirming all manifestations of the Great Reason, thou art the bestower of joy of cosmic creativeness. The Ruleress will adorn the aspiring realm with creative fire. Ruleress of thought, thou who invokest life, to Thee We make manifest the radiance of Our Ray. Mother, venerated of the Lords, We carry in Our Heart the fire of Thy Love. In Thy Heart lives the ordaining Ray. In Thy Heart life is conceived, and We shall affirm the Ray of the Ruleress. Yes, yes, yes!

Thus the Cosmos lives in the greatness of the two Origins. Yes, yes, yes! Thus the Cosmos crowns the two Origins. Thus the Mother of the World and the Lords build life. Yes, yes, yes! And in boundless striving the Cosmic Magnet welds its sacred parts. Thus, We venerate the Ruleress beyond all spheres.

10. Vast is the field for the manifested approaching Tara. We, the Arhats, ascending to the Fire of Space, prostrate Ourselves before the entire Fiery Bosom of the Mother of the World. The Bosom of the Mother of the World finds all reflections upon Earth. One of them, the most powerful and the most intense, is the advent of the coming Tara. The Mother of the World carries visibly and invisibly the manifestation of those ineffable threads—the affirmation of the world's threads.

Let us find the reflection of the Cosmos in the great principle of construction and fusion. When the Brothers of Humanity feel sorrow over the Image in which they are held by the human consciousness, they can only say, "You are building your hypotheses upon apparent phantoms. We are only phantoms for humanity! When the spirit affirms Our Flaming Existence, then, instead of phantoms, We shall become the Fiery Warriors."

11. To the Brothers of Humanity is assigned the construction of the life of the planet; and they maintain the Command of the great Mother of the World. The music of the spheres resounds when the current of joy is in motion. The music of the spheres fills space when the heart is stirred to tremor by the cosmic force. The Heart of Our Brotherhood safeguards for humanity the path to the General Good.

12. Humanity has never deliberated upon the life of the Arhat. It is customary to think of an Arhat as a dweller of the clouds. The records of the drift of thought are dreadful and grotesque. Verily, We Brothers of Humanity do not recognize ourselves as humanity conceives Us. The images of Us are so fantastic that We deem that if people applied their fantasies precisely conversely, Our Images would assume true form.

The karmic tie apparently disappears when human thought pictures an Arhat. Everything takes on a new dimension. Everything becomes improbable. Everything becomes uncorrelated to reality. Let us say, in proceeding to the higher worlds, that an Arhat is limitless in all manifestations. In ascending, an Arhat elevates along with himself all the highest and most subtle energies.

We can show Our true Images only to near ones. We can send Our Rays only to near ones. Yes, yes, yes!

13. If it were possible to impart Our Image to humanity, the striving toward knowledge would be established. Of course it would be necessary to impart the Image over a span of millenniums. The "Book of

Life" is beautiful in its complete affirmation. Assuredly, when it is possible to impart the complete picture of the Cosmic Magnet, then the manifestation of the beauty of Existence is affirmed.

If it were possible to impart the entire picture of the whole path of an Arhat's course of lives, then Our Image would take on its true aspect. The "Book of Our Life" resounds mightily and cements Our step.

Each Lord has his keynote. The Epoch of Maitreya proclaims woman. The manifestation of Maitreya is linked with the confirmation of the Mother of the World, in the past, present, and future. The "Book of Life" is so beautiful.

14. Much has been spoken about Man-God aspiring toward deification. Many are the memorable records citing the Images striving toward higher worlds. But how dimly are they formulated in the human consciousness! Man-God is to man only one who departed to other worlds! But We Brothers of Humanity seek and proclaim Man-God on Earth. We revere all Images, but none more than the great Image of Man-God, who bears in his heart the full Chalice, ready for flight, but bearing his full Chalice on Earth. Renouncing his destiny, he strains his fiery being. In the fulfillment of his destiny man confirms the Cosmic Magnet. Man-God is a fiery creator. Man-God is the carrier of the fiery sign of the New Race. Man-God is aflame with all fires. Thus, inscribe in the records about Man-God: Arhat, Agni Yogi, Tara—so shall We inscribe.

15. Man-God advances as an evident aspiring Redeemer of Humanity. We guard this sacred truth about Man-God. I affirm that the Tara, carrying the flaming Chalice of aspirations for the redemption of humanity, can proclaim Our manifestation among

men. The origin of the power of the Cosmic Magnet bestows striving toward the consummation. We Brothers of Humanity point out that the change will take place through the fiery principle. Verily, Our new step is so beautiful! The currents of the higher spheres impel the currents toward the construction of Our Cosmic force. Great is the attraction! When striving hearts aspire toward consummation, the impetuosity increases, and the current of oneness is affirmed by the tension of the Cosmic Magnet. Thus the union resounds.

16. The prayer uttered by Christ when leaving Earth was not heard by people. The prayer uttered by Buddha was not heard by people. The prayer that will be uttered by Maitreya knocks like lightning at the gates of the human spirit. Thus is Earth stratified and the consciousness of the spirit created.

When the dates approach, the work of creativeness may be entered upon. The creativeness of the Origins maintains a rhythm, neither retarding nor hastening.

Along with the planetary life there proceeds the construction for the higher spheres. The sweep of the constructiveness of the spirit completing its planetary life is so complex that one may truly call it a "dual constructiveness," and the spirit is the guide in life. On the last step the spirit cannot affirm itself in the existing forms; a striving toward new forms to a very great extent fills the consciousness and the spirit.

The existing forms correspond very little to the beauty of the future. I testify that there are many mysteries in the life of an attained Arhat.

17. How little does humanity ponder over the idea of responsibility, when the concept of Shambhala is regarded by people as a land ordained for rest. If people would only realize that the Brothers of Humanity

bear all the burden of man's consciousness! If people would realize that We carry the responsibility for their schemes! If people would realize that, in essence, Shambhala is the Source which creates a new and better step for humanity!

When I say that the suffusing of the earthly crust is Our task, man should understand that Our planet must arouse itself. Cosmos awaits!

People plead for Good. The Cosmos affirms humanity not as the manifestation of one who receives, but as a receiving creator. Thus is the step laid, and the spirit of a creator can construct powerfully when the might of tension reaches to the summits of Cosmos.

18. The comprehension of Our Image by humanity is entirely contrary to reality. When Our Images live in the consciousness as Those who are responsible for humanity, We can accept this spirit as one who understands the tensed heart of an Arhat. Certainly We must say that in Our creative work We are moved by the one feeling of law. But the conceptions of law are so varied! When We Brothers of Humanity speak of law as the stimulus of Our existence, We definitely speak of the great law of the Magnet. In Our law the entire cosmic life, premised upon the great attraction, is transformed. The attraction has, in its striving, the greatest heart. Your law is based on human cruelty; Our law is based upon the Heart of the Mother of the World.

19. Upon this planet exists a manifestation closely approaching the constructiveness on the far-off worlds. For millenniums We have been cultivating this manifestation. And thus are We Brothers of Humanity striving to Our powers of Hierarchy. By the same Magnet We are striving to the very Power which exalts Our creativeness. Wondrous is the predestination of Our existence! Upholding the Chalice of manifestations, one can be manifested as a power; both hands are outstretched to the Chalice.

20. One may understand that page of Our constructions as the intensified Magnet. Humanity, in accepting the Magnet and its intensified action, must also accept the ever increasing power of the Magnet as the evidence of the Lord's Hand. Of the act of creativeness, I may say that each spirit creates individually. Spirit-creativeness is so powerful that, even when the memory does not recall its actions, it can create an affirmation of the most difficult task.

21. We say "the arc of consciousness," because We term the consciousness of an Arhat a complete circle. But there is a still higher step of cognition; We call it "full affirmation." The Cosmic Magnet is Our Sacred Power. Boundless is the immensity of this Power. If only the spirit would manifest understanding, fearlessness would suffuse all hearts, and the spheres would resound with rejoicing.

The Arhat proceeds, carrying the power of the Cosmic Magnet in his heart! Cosmos creates; it creates the beauty of Be-ness. I can call striving a cosmic magnet.

22. In the creativeness of an Arhat the heart manifests that striving which is attested by the Cosmic Magnet through educing intensified combinations. The actual creative tension of the striving heart of an Arhat is so aflame with the Fire of Space!

To bring about the advance of evolution, to bestow affirmed truth and knowledge, and to link humanity with the currents of evolution—this stimulus inspires each move of an Arhat. This tension sets into motion all feelings and subtle energies. Thus proceeds the manifested Friend of humanity. These spatial strivings are the foundations of Our cooperation. Similarly sustained are the centers of the fiery Agni Yogi as a friend of humanity. Yes, yes, yes! Thus We serve the progress of humanity.

23. You heard correctly about sovereign power. Verily, the Hierarch uses the power for cosmic progress. We Brothers of Humanity possess this power of acting in step with the Cosmic Magnet. I attest, verily, that We create by a strained heart. Thus let us understand unity. The cosmic creativeness also achieves in being strained by the Heart of Reason. Yes, yes, yes! This law is the attestation of Reason. Only thus does Cosmos create. Yes, yes, yes!

To Thee, Mother of the World, the law of Existence is made manifest. To Thee, Ruleress, We Brothers of Humanity pay reverence. Thee, Thee, Thee! Thus the unified heart rules in the Universe. Yes, yes, yes!

24. Man is merciless to himself. Bewailing his fate, he forgets that he inflicts upon himself a severe penalty. It is difficult for Us to make people assimilate the thought of karma; but in a still more intractable state is the consciousness of a man headed straight for the abyss. People prefer self-destruction and self-deception to the enlightenment of consciousness.

The quest for Shambhala varies widely in the spiritual domain. And is it possible that people believe they will attain the Community of Shambhala through invasion or through fasting? To him who is aware of the path to Us, let us say, "Walk by the path of love. Walk by the path of labor. Walk by the path of the shield of faith!" To him who has found Our Image in his heart, We shall say, "Walk by the way of the heart and the Chalice will affirm the path!" To him who, through conceit, thinks he has attained the path, We shall say, "Go and learn from the spirit who knows consummation."

The little girl carrying the heavy volume of the Bible in the chambers of luxury appears as a creator of a new world. The little girl who perceived the Teacher of Light under the blue sky is the destroyer of the dungeons of darkness. When the spirit of a small girl could feel the Brothers of Humanity, then the name of this spirit is a light-bearing sword. When, since childhood, the spirit could sense that the Brothers of Humanity regenerate that which exists, then this spirit holds the light-bearing name. We cherish the spiritual leaders among children.

The evidence of enlightenment is the best gift to evolution. The Command of cosmic life is a summons to light-sustaining achievement, and this mission is affirmed only by Light.

25. The stream of karma rushes like a torrent, and consciousness may transform this tide into a repeated sacred union of beauty. But the way in which people understand the karmic stream is attested in human deeds. The evidence of the affirmation of karma and of union is attested by Us as the greatest Truth.

26. The subtlety of Our Indications to humanity is not yet comprehended. When will it be possible to illumine man with Our Image? The tendency of thought comprehends only with difficulty the purity of the higher sphere. Sacredly We guard the Sacrament of Life. The wheel of life breathes with beauty. The wheel of life is suffused by the grandeur of Cosmos. The wheel of life is directed toward the greatness of Materia Lucida. And equally light-sustaining are the rays of each manifestation of life that merges into the immensity of Cosmos. The sacred bonds of spirit are comparable to the most light-sustaining rays. The atomic energy of karma, consciously woven, comprises the most powerful lever.

27. Verily, the tortuous line of the spirit retards its growth. A spasmodic striving induces an explosion which rends space. Each striving wave leads to creativeness. Each descending action induces an explosion. The most awful action is the rejection of the given Decrees. On the way to the Brotherhood one must understand that the highest Hierarch has his entrusted ones. Therefore, none should deny that which is given through Our entrusted ones, otherwise the higher steps will be inaccessible. Therefore I will repeat this until the consciousness is imbued with the greatest principle. Hence you, denying ones, guard this treasure that is given you for ascent!

28. Beautiful is the thought about Brotherhood upon Earth. Each disciplining of spirit produces striving. Only the will can give discipline to the spirit. But when the thought rambles, asserting selfhood, then verily there is no channel for true vital action. Every applied thought will bring growth to the spirit. Thus, each applied thought of the Tara and the Guru will further the expansion of consciousness. Thus, only the Chain of Hierarchy will give the possibility of ascent. Complete obedience leads to true creativeness, for when obedience guides the action, power increases, and the pledge strains all forces.

29. He who adheres to the Teaching of Infinity gains freedom of action first of all. He who fears to adhere to the Brotherhood deprives himself of the Highest. He who dreads dogma can strengthen himself in the Teaching as in flight to the far-off worlds. He who dreads such communion can remain at the threshold. Incessancy of striving affords affirmation of Our Teaching.

The Arhats, who bestow on humanity the concept of the full Chalice, cannot deprive humanity of freedom. Not in renunciation or in seclusion does the Brotherhood dwell. Each spark that kindles the consciousness is recorded; each striving arrow is recorded. Not abstraction, but fiery striving endures. Those who know the attainment of cosmic strivings may verily say, "We create with fire. We strive with fire. We live in fire. Not miracles these, but the transmutation of life into the garment of Materia Lucida."

How does the Brotherhood live? How does the Brotherhood act? From Our Abode the threads of Our creativeness are stretched to the hearts, as inspirations to humanity.

30. The thought of obedience to a Teacher is foreign to humanity. But how can a spirit not succeed when the Teacher is the Leading Beacon? How can the disciple lose his fire when the Teacher is the kindler of all fires? How can the Shield of the Teacher be an obstacle to the disciple when it is the Teacher who impels his fiery striving? In the consciousness of humanity lives a germinal desire to strive for a common work that leads all forward, in unity. But humanity must learn independent action, and must implement the affirmed thoughts of the Teacher. Thus does human evolution achieve harmony with Cosmic Reason. Humanity must learn to create by the higher way.

Truly, emulation of the Teacher is the taking of the Image of the Teacher into one's heart.

31. The realization of goal-fitness is a token of cooperation with Us. How else can one gain an understanding of the Magnets sent to different countries? How else can one approach the manifestation of the magnetization of human consciousness, which in silence attracts the eyes of an entire nation to itself? Thus one can trace how Our commissioned Sisters and Brothers have attracted and revolved around themselves the consciousness of entire nations. But for this one must vigilantly understand the value of each step.

32. How can we achieve a comprehension of the Magnet if we doubt the Indications of the Lord? How can we conquer an enemy if we doubt the power granted to us? How can we expect to build anything strong if we do not accept the irrevocable Indications of Hierarchy?

33. How can one come close to the Source? How will the higher understanding be affirmed? Only by the law of Hierarchy. The Guiding Hand is the Uplifting Hand. The Indicating Hand is the Hand revealing the path to the Highest Law. Thus is created the great step of the law of Hierarchy. Truly!

34. Only matured spirits can burden themselves with the knowledge of exact dates. It is impossible to imagine how many strings have been broken by the presumption of dates. The efforts of even valiant spirits have often been impeded by the barrier of dates. It is useful to know the direction, but a limited date impedes the cosmic constructiveness. How can one speak of Magnets when each date will divide the thread of a progressive movement? Only vigilance and goal-fitness will lead without wasting energy.

35. How do people understand the law of Hierarchy? How do they fulfill its laws in life? How do they intensify the best striving in themselves? Truly the law of Hierarchy is mistakenly understood as an individual's right; it is forgotten that a Hierarch is a Link in a Chain, and One who fulfills the Will of an even Higher One. Only by knowing this is it possible to properly respond to the higher mission. Only thus can one validate the Trust and build the fiery accumulations in the Chalice.

36. Thus the appointment of a Hierarch is the

appointment of One who fulfills the Higher Will. When the spirit assigns to himself the affirmed right, he can achieve only through the fulfillment of the Higher Command.

37. Remember the laws of gravitation and repulsion, action and counteraction. Steadfastness results from attraction, and tension from repulsion. Attraction along the line of Hierarchy leads to Me, and repulsion from the enemy to glorification. Thus, the Teacher and the enemy are cornerstones.

The trainer of wild animals must first excite their rage before he succeeds in taming them. No motion is possible without tension; therefore, every progressive Teaching needs its enemies and its Teacher. One must keep in mind the physical law in order to understand the immutability of the law of the spirit. My Advice is that the significance of the Teacher and the need for enemies must be understood. Certainly, only the Teacher will lead the enemy to fury. The full measure of evil must be manifested before one may rise regenerated out of the flames of wrath. It is impossible to avoid the obstacles of the path, but know that no obstructive tensions will occur without being of benefit. Indeed they may be of service to entire nations!

If a hermit is able with his thought alone to destroy a stronghold of evil, then the tensity that is allowed by the Higher Forces will be like a battering ram against the hostile forces.

38. Each growth of spirit requires burdening through circumstances. There exists an ancient legend that out of human sufferings are created precious stones. Thus it is, and when I say, "Burden Me," it does not mean that I bring a sacrifice, I am only multiplying the power of the spirit. Likewise, people must realize how much closer the latest discoveries bring them to the solution of cosmic problems. For every call flashes throughout the worlds; and as the ordinary photographic apparatus can make a print of the astral world, so every wave of any current can unite the threads of the far-off worlds.

It is time to understand the responsibility and the privilege afforded by earthly incarnations. Yet people often avoid listening to the waves of space and catching the echoes and answers which come from various strata of the Universe. We are repeating about the privileges of spiritual development, but the matter is so distorted that a well-meaning denizen even fears to mention anything that is linked with the radiant region of spirit. Try to speak of the light of realization and the bliss of spirit and you will be feared like robbers and murderers. But even robbers were disciples of Christ and Buddha; hence do not fear human epithets, but harken to the Voice of Eternity, which leads to Bliss and Light.

Fear not, fear not, fear not!

39. The creativeness of Cosmos is always built through the tension of all energies. For all achievements the quality of energies should be affirmed. Therefore, the higher the tension, the more powerful is the manifestation of victory. Our creativeness is saturated with the quality of power. Therefore, having gathered all energies, we can rely upon success. Only the quality of energies gives the needed standard of labor. Therefore it is so important to have an expanded consciousness and to embrace all that is needed for constructiveness.

40. In fulfilling My Will you offer Me the opportunity to fulfill your will. Where is the boundary between wills that together strive toward Light? One may remember that We lead those who have entrusted themselves to Us along the paths of well-tested magnets. One can trust a Helmsman who has already sailed the oceans.

"Cross the bridge. Test thyself. But My Star has known the ages."

Fear will not touch the well-tested heart.

41. The quality of action is forged by striving. When words are turned into action, the higher energy is affirmed. Only in life can one manifest the higher energies. Not words but actions are considered to be the affirmation of the higher energies. Only when the potential of the spirit is manifested in action can concordance with the Highest be affirmed.

Thus, a striving quest provides the key to the Infinite.

42. Therefore Our Plan is so mighty. Therefore Our Teaching is so powerful because Our Words enter into life as wondrous affirmations. Thus do Our Words live, for the creative impulse is saturated by the power of Fire. Only when Our Teaching is applied in life can the higher step be taken.

Why is your mission so effective? Because it carries within it Our pledge of Cooperation. Thus We affirm Hierarchy based upon the law of succession. When the Cosmic Law is realized, a true understanding of the Chain of Hierarchy is established. Thus, the one who better fulfills his tasks will be closer to Hierarchy. The Hierarchy of Service is but the manifestation of the fulfillment of the Higher Will.

43. Through what means is the spirit transformed? Through the creativity of the impulse. Through what does the spirit ascend? By the creativity of striving. How, then, can the spirit fail to be saturated with fire if only thus is one able to join the Cosmic Magnet? But the consciousness of the Higher Spirit indeed is saturated fire! Therefore only the realization of the Higher Will can lead the spirit toward its goal. Thus each consciously-taken step lends beauty to action. Creativity that adheres to the affirmed fire is magnetized through conscious fulfillment of the Higher Will.

44. Therefore, each thought put into action is a contribution to the fiery creativeness. Each fulfilled thought is linked to Our actions. How carefully must the disciples examine the quality of their thoughts! Has not the worm of egoism, or conceit, or the manifestation of self-love hidden somewhere? The ability to admit this honestly is something that each spirit must develop within himself. Only thus can one fulfill one's mission in the Plan of the Lords.

The Chain of Hierarchy is built by fulfillment of the Higher Will.

45. The quality of thought is so powerful that the Fire of Space responds to the tension of thought. The cosmic affirmation can take place only when a corresponding harmony is established. Thus each correspondence brings its consequences. The warrant of the broadening of consciousness lies in the development of sensitiveness. Hence, the quality of striving is the truest indicator of the growth of the spirit; and consciousness is manifested as the affirmed power of creativeness.

46. Thus, the quality of thought is intensified by the impulse of search. The creativeness of spirit is intensified by the power of fire. Therefore, Our workers must realize the entire power of creative thought and kindle their fires. Thus, only the quality of thought can broaden the consciousness. Thus let Our workers remember.

47. One yogi gained the reputation of being a practical joker because unnoticeably he moved various objects in people's houses, and when asked why, answered, "I am checking to see if you have become blind." Truly, there are few who notice changes in their surroundings. But the first sign of an "eagle-eye" is the ability to notice the smallest changes, since on them depends the vibration of the whole.

48. Certainly the power of Hierarchy is the most vital, and only by this bridge can one build. Thus, in the foundation of each great beginning is laid the energy imbued by the law of Hierarchy. Only upon the principle of harmony and unification can one build. Only upon the basis of affirmation of the principle of Hierarchy can higher possibilities be affirmed. The Creative Will proclaims that a united consciousness leads to harmonious decisions.

49. Attentiveness can be tested in a simple way. Move an object to a new place; if it remains unnoticed, do the same with a larger object and observe what "elephant" finally attracts the "sharp" eye. Test yourself and others. Test for fear, for irritation, and for laziness—and for all failings that cause the litmus paper to blush with shame. There is no need of complicated invocations, since simple attentiveness moves one many steps further. Thus one should begin to develop the "eagle-eye."

50. Harmonious sendings bring much usefulness, especially when one dominant tone can be followed, as for a musical key. A primary note may even be struck with a tuning fork. A magnet, a tuning fork, a ring, and many common devices easily enter into the daily life of the young yogis. The clearing away of accumulations of debris requires the use of shovel and broom. One should not fear everyday objects—as below, so above.

It is wise to become accustomed to there being no

rest or end. But the realization alone of Hierarchy and Our Brotherhood already directs the traveler along the shortest path in the Infinite.

51. The orbit that attracts conscious strivings will always bring the spirit to Our Gates. The creativeness of spirit resounds throughout all space, and only acknowledgment of Higher Might imbues the spirit with creative searching. Thus, each orbit that attracts one to higher creativeness is imbued with all the highest energies. Only the path of conscious quest affords striving toward Our Orbit. Thus one may attain the upper steps.

52. Do not accustom the young ones to expect great manifestations according to their human measure. Such an outworn measure does not correspond to reality, for even in a physical sense people have greatly distorted the concept of immensity. The mind cannot comprehend that only the result defines the true grandeur. Each action can be measured only in accordance with its relation to Hierarchy and Infinity. Thus, these concepts will be like signs leading to reality. Hence, teach the young ones to think first of Infinity, remembering, moreover, that no one should compare himself to a minute grain of sand as is usually the way of hypocrites. Our measure is guaranteed by an immense responsibility. We shall not err in measuring according to responsibility.

53. During the construction of the designated undertakings it should be remembered that construction always progresses onward. During a construction in the name of the Lord there is only one way that brings us to the Creative Source—the way of the mighty Hierarchy, the path of the powerful guidance of the Great Service. Therefore, adhering to the creative principle impels the spirit to the affirmed law of

Hierarchy. Each construction requires the realization of upward striving. Hence, only the law of obedience to Hierarchy can give a legitimate tensity. Only thus can one realize the path leading to the mighty Infinity.

54. The legend about the giant supporting Earth is not a superstition, but a memory of Him who assumed the burden of responsibility for Earth. Thus, in each action there is one who has taken the responsibility upon his shoulders. The one in cooperation with others constitutes the balance. Like a spinning top, the rhythm of motion should be kept; thus mechanics is transformed into art. The display of simple attentiveness, which We pointed out first in legends and symbols, I now ordain in a simple Command—merely open your eyes, because there are many signs around.

55. The filling of the Chalice determines the quality of action. Each thought leading to the mighty understanding of Hierarchy uplifts the spirit. Therefore, as striving grows, the broadening of consciousness leads the spirit to the understanding of the Origins. Creativeness of the spirit can build a bridge to higher understanding only through the subtlest energies. Therefore, the accumulation in the Chalice gives the best possibilities and attainments. Man must strive to fill the Chalice and expand the consciousness. Thus, the subtlest energies are within reach of only the subtlest receptivity, and limitless striving opens the Gates to Beauty.

56. Certainly, when the spirit is accustomed to respond in Service in conformity with higher predestinations, the link of the spirit with the Higher Will is established. Hence, one should apply one's striving to perception of the Higher Will. Only thus can a Hierarch serve Our task. Verily adoption and fulfillment are the valor of a Hierarch. Therefore, I affirm that the power of creativeness is in the blending of consciousnesses. Thus We create the predestined future. I affirm it!

57. Mean thoughts have been compared to crawling reptiles. Nothing is more analogous to this scum of the consciousness. Can one sit calmly in an armchair, knowing that beneath him crawl poisonous snakes and scorpions? One must free oneself from reptiles, and primarily on the path to Hierarchy. Condemnation of and blasphemy against the Lord are irreparable. Thus, each one who condemns the Hierarch must remember that his levity and crime will infect his karma for many ages. Verily, if there is only one way—through the Lord—to the one Light, then only extreme ignorance will allow destruction of this single path. One must assert striving to the Highest as the essence of life and assume a reverent attitude toward this salutary striving. By belittling the Hierarch one may condemn oneself and inflict perilous harm on many near ones. It is time to remember this!

58. When space is being clouded by the mist of non-understanding, then it is certainly difficult for the creative rays to penetrate. Each layer is permeated in conformity with the complex of its striving. Therefore, the earthly layers are so impenetrable. Hence, all quests of the spirit must proceed in a tense tempo. The quests of the spirit must attract it to the Magnet of Hierarchy, since each power has its correspondence upon Earth. Thus the law of Hierarchy must be applied vitally.

59. Some people pour a daily gruel over the Image of the Teacher and imagine themselves to be in the Great Service. The Teaching and Service presuppose first of all the expansion of consciousness on the basis of adherence to the Teaching and reverence for the Teacher. In studying Infinity one should first of all

realize the limitlessness of love and devotion. It is not wise to say that love has overflowed and devotion has withered, because the consequence will be the disintegration of one's self. One should understand the limitlessness of love and devotion as the first steps toward Service and Yoga. One should set oneself this task, at least as a means of one's own progress. One should advance only in the direction of the Teacher. Then, only, does relief come. But making a daily onion gruel out of the Teacher will not lead to success. Sacredly, limitlessly, let us sustain our love and reverence for the Teacher, as a healing means of regeneration.

60. The prayer of the heart is the expression of love and devotion. Let us fill our vessel of experiences, because inevitably we must come to it. Let us not waste precious time in demeaning and in dissolution. Each dissolution evokes unbridled elements, in other words, it opposes the manifested Cosmos. The growth of consciousness is verily Our festival.

61. When thought comprises striving toward the fulfillment of the Higher Will, a direct connection with the Shield of the Higher Will is established. Can one reach an understanding of Cosmos without striving to penetrate into the Higher Spheres? Only succession gives foundation to all strivings. All that exists proceeds by the law of succession. Hence, each isolation results only in the loss of the predestined. Thus, thought is generated as the carrier of the law of succession. Thus the law of the Higher Will creates limitlessly.

62. In all religions the one departing from Earth has been accorded an accompanying Intercessor in the aspect of a saint, angel, or departed relative. Thus was affirmed the existence of a world beyond the grave and the need of a Guide. One should become accustomed to this thought of the need of a Guide. Thus in all religions the Guide and the Teacher were affirmed. Hence when We speak of the Teacher, We remind of that which is inevitable. The Teaching can live, or turn into the embrace of death. But it is easy to enhance life by turning to Light.

63. The assertion of a correct decision is the property of psychic energy. Then how greatly must men develop this property in themselves! Without this property one cannot assimilate the Fire of Space. Without this property one cannot receive the preordained treasure. Only contact with the Higher can give the direction; therefore it is necessary to strive to an understanding of the Higher Principle. Only thus shall we approach the law of Hierarchy.

64. Only the reflex of the reflexes of psychic energy can be perceived through physical sensations. The same may be said of subtle energies and the remote bodies of Cosmos. But that should not discourage researches, because by the shadow and the source of light one can define the height of an object. All Western methods of ascertainment can also be applied, for I do not see any difference between the West and the East when we are at the summits of research. It is necessary by every means to dissolve all the conventional divisions of ignorance. Let us not be afraid to investigate by all methods—only learn to know!

65. The qualities of actions testify to the decisiveness of striving. Each action is imbued with its own essence. The impulse of motion compels one to ascertain the impetus of an achievement. The quality of the action determines the quality of the affirmation. Then how must the spirit strive to the refinement of the essence and quality of action! The entire pledge of creativeness and the direction of action are contained in the trend of thought. Therefore the approach to the Chain of Hierarchy directs the spirit toward the truth of creativeness. Thus one should seek to fulfill the Higher Will.

66. Humanity's alienation from the understanding of fulfillment of the Higher Will has placed humanity in a position that has segregated it. Therefore Our disciples have to apply their whole strength for the fulfillment, in order not to isolate themselves. Hence it is so important to understand the law of Hierarchy.

67. You can perform one of the most useful psychic experiments. If you accept all Our Counsels and it seems to you that something indicated was not fulfilled or was not transmitted in accordance with your expectations, then immediately study the Counsel itself, applying the words in accordance with the customary human understanding; then recall all the circumstances that have taken place and consider all your own thoughts, worries, irritation, and all accompanying hazards and blunders. It is very significant to observe the events that have influence over the cosmic waves. One may see that however ponderous is our human burden, it cannot be compared to the minutest thought. In this way you can observe to what degree the psychic sphere has its own laws, beyond our three dimensions.

Beginning with such observations, one can arrive at valuable conclusions which, when accumulated, will bring great benefits to humanity. Because the time has now arrived for especially keen application of the psychic laws. It is time to gather into the chalice of patience all the designs and to remember that each fluctuation of climate and atmospheric pressures also exerts its deep influence upon the psychic laws. Let us apply the most precise scale for weighing our thoughts, and let us remember that each oxidization of metals exerts influence upon the character and quality of thoughts. Smoke, and also the odor of burning refuse or meat, is always harmful. Let us not forget that dust, like particles of decay, penetrates the pores of the body. Let us calmly discriminate in all the details of life, not for self-vindication, but for the investigation of our nature and acceptance of the measures of perfection.

68. One more significant experiment: Accustom yourselves to see without looking and to hear without listening. That is, you must be able to aim your vision into the spiritual realms to a degree that, in spite of open eyes, you will not see that which is before you, and in spite of open ears, you will not hear evident noise. Through such physical tests one can greatly progress in psychic vision and hearing. For this, it is useful to hold constantly in imagination before oneself the Image of the Teacher as that which is the most precious to bind you with the Supreme.

Now, imagine for a moment that you have succeeded, with the help of chemical reactions, in creating a complete microcosm; for this microcosm you are the creator! Then why is it so difficult for people to imagine an endless chain of Creators from the lowest to the Highest, up to the Inaccessible?

Therefore, in speaking of the Infinite, we will not imagine it as something void or measureless, but as something integral in its incessant ascent. And is not the entire Infinite expressed in your consciousness, for where are the measure and boundaries of your consciousness? Thus, from the smallest to the Greatest, proceed by steps, each link being visible and tangible. There the indicated experiment will serve you in seeing through the physical, impenetrable forms which stand before you. From the evident proceed to the reality that will enrich your path.

69. Another useful exercise: Try to write different things with both hands at the same time. Or try to dictate two letters or conduct two conversations at the same time. Try to drive a motor car and carry on a conversation about complicated problems at the same time. Try to refrain from quarrels when the changeable mood of your companion invites your irritation. Try numerous examples of dividing your consciousness. Try to pour your energy in several directions without losing its value or weakening its flow.

A one-sided effort is related to Kali Yuga. But the streams of all energies, like a salutary current, will enrich the discoveries of Satya Yuga. In past centuries we have had examples of the successful division of consciousness. But now we should especially affirm the action of all channels of Brahmavidya.

Pay attention to the flow of thoughts and affirm the right waves of rhythm. People should not become like animals, who can think only in one direction at a time. The Sons of Light and Flame should sparkle in full freedom and kindle the fires of space. Verily the time comes for the kindling of the fires of space, in other words, for their manifestation even in the nearest physical sphere. It is a difficult time when fires can flash out and, if undisciplined, can burn and annihilate.

Accept these reminders as the lesson of the day. Do not consider that in heaven there are different laws and that we are still preserved through ignorance of lower matter. Indeed not. You know, and you will begin to apply all counsels.

70. Aerolites are not sufficiently studied, and still less attention is accorded to the cosmic dust upon the eternal snows and glaciers. However, the Cosmic

Ocean designs its rhythm on the summits. If we begin to think of Infinity, we should pay attention primarily to all that comes from beyond and links us materially with the far-off worlds. How, then, can one venture upon a distant voyage without paying attention to the guests from afar? Also, symptoms of life upon the eternal snows should be compared with those upon the plains. Perhaps the excessive growth of certain glands is caused by the use of water from the snows, which causes a disorder resulting from the action of the particles of cosmic dust. So many useful observations are diffused around us, one must only stretch out one's hand!

You have also correctly remarked that the majority of tubercular cases are nothing else but the kindling of the centers of the lungs. Certainly, the fires that have been stored up by karma, but not realized or applied, may become destructive.

71. One may prosecute ignorance, but one should especially chastise superstition and hypocrisy. Like a leprous film, superstition covers weak brains. We are not against laboratories and Western methods, but We ask that honesty, efficiency, and the courage of impartiality be added to them. How can one think of cooperation when birdlike brains impede each experiment? One can produce the most stupendous manifestation if the horns of the devil do not impede in the test tube. People believe more in devils than in saints!

72. Each striving is saturated with the fire of spirit. The creativeness of the spirit takes part in the fiery constructiveness of the Cosmos. How can one be isolated from the entire cosmic creativeness when man is the creative fulfiller of the Cosmic Will! One should therefore develop in oneself consonance with the Higher Forces, for without striving to consonance there is no creativeness. Thus, humanity must be affirmed in the understanding of the Higher Forces and adhere to the Higher Will.

73. Certainly one can attain only through adherence to Hierarchy. Only the understanding of the great law will open the eyes of humanity. How, then, not to penetrate into the might of constructiveness? Therefore, Our disciples must be imbued with an understanding of the affirmation of Hierarchy. Therefore, one can build only when Our Carriers of Fire carry Our Will and the disciples accept that which is sent. Each builder knows the law of Hierarchy.

74. Upon investigation, the quality of thought belongs to the category of subtlest energies. It is impossible to measure the fluctuation of thought, therefore We have established the probation of disciples by the refinement of thought. Every three years We give the disciple the possibility of expressing himself in regard to the same event. Only according to these dates can one see the fluctuation of selfhood, cooperation, patience, and devotion. Similar experiments can be applied to other manifestations of energies; the more so since people have completely forgotten about probations. One can also test oneself, directing one's attention to old objects and observing the reaction of the influence of remembrance. Likewise one can test oneself upon flowers, music, upon a book read long ago. One can scientifically observe the influence of surroundings upon an object long since familiar. How many steps could be counted forward or backward! Besides, one can ponder why a step crossed for the second time is always much more difficult.

75. Certainly, an experiment upon oneself is always useful because it reminds one of probation. Probation is the sign of creativeness. One must get accustomed

to the thought that men create unceasingly. With each glance, with each breath, with each motion they change the course of the cosmic waves. Since there is no vacuum, how, then, are the worlds linked? The cells of life grow like the leaves of a tree. But we forget that the mold of each of our motions remains. How beautiful it must be in order to be worthy of the Great Builder!

76. Cosmic creativeness is based upon conformity. Without the law of conformity it is impossible to affirm creativeness and the development of fiery receptivity. Hence it is so important to apply this essential law to life. Verily, without the power of conformity and fiery receptivity it is impossible to bring about the predestined.

77. Each step requires new circumstances. Each new step brings its affirmed power. Therefore in the midst of the difficult time a mighty step in conformity with the difficulties is being laid. Hence the creative activity of Our co-workers will bring the manifestation of success when thoughts shall be affirmed upon the might of the future. Thus We build a wondrous step! Thus We build amidst the dissolution of the countries! Thus Our Power enters into life! The manifestation of a new step is so close, but the world decides its fate.

78. Nothing is neglected in the world. Sometimes we measure by great scales, but often experiments with small units should be performed. The trend of thought should likewise be observed. The giants of thought are as instructive as the small leeches. One may see someone who has overcome a tremendous obstacle stumbling over an insignificant puddle. Rancor, offense, thought of self destroy the possibilities just as do treason and fear. One must discriminate the circumstances; where is the new touchstone? Thus, with

sharp-sightedness we reach the realization of joy for each probation. We shall say, "Lord, send Thy Will—give or take. Together with Thee, we shall examine my pitfalls. Together we shall deliberate my decisions of yesterday. Today I am satisfied, and Thou, better than I, knowest the quantity of nurture needed for the morrow. I shall not transgress Thy Will, because only from Thy Hand can I receive." Thus, one must watch oneself in the great and in the small.

79. Already you know how tense is the time; and to those who are seized with fear, say that when the Lord lives within the heart, no hair will fall from one's head, and to each one a palace for body and spirit is allotted. But preserve your heart in purity, in order that I may enter there and surround you with armor. Remember that if you give in spirit to the Lord what has been taken from you, He will reward you a hundredfold. Thus, direct your thought to the Lord and let the Lord enter your heart. Without the Lord it will be narrow in the empty heart, and, like peas in a dried sheepskin, wrath will jar within the empty heart. Fill your heart with the Lord so fully that no enemy can force his way through. Peace unto you.

80. The attraction of corresponding forces is saturated with striving which unites the forces. The affirmation of all shiftings is intensified by energies which function according to the law of correspondence. Therefore each creative force is subject to this law. Cosmic creativeness depends on these correspondences. Hence We intensify all forces and affirm the highest correspondence. Thus the Chain of Hierarchy builds lawfully the steps of correspondence, and each striving is saturated with a subtle response. Only concordance can affirm a limitless creativeness.

81. It will be asked, How must we direct our

prayers to the Highest One if the Image of the Lord is constantly before us? Say, Precisely through Him address yourself to the Highest One. Besides, if you have reached the state of keeping a constant Image of the Lord before you, this question cannot disquiet you at all. When we reach a conscious communion with the subtlest energies, much of that which did not find its place yesterday becomes fully comprehensible today. Thus we learn to rejoice and to be calm, where yesterday we sorrowed. It is useful to observe how our consciousness is purified through everyday labor. Now especially the tempering of these swords is timely, because the air is filled with fire. Only the Image of the Lord can rotate all centers and serve as a Shield. Let us not be afraid to repeat about swords and shields, because We desire peace and the reign of spirit. As victors cease to remember their enemies, so We do not count them; and a forest will not suffice to liken them to trees.

82. The Sons of Reason—We proclaim them as Hierarchs upon Earth. The Daughters of Reason—thus, also, We proclaim them upon Earth. Those who strive to the evolution of the spirit must follow in the steps of Hierarchy in order to progress. Who, then, will nurture the spirit of striving disciples? Who, then, will affirm the path of ascent? Only the Daughters and Sons of Reason. In whom are contained the fires of attainment? In the Daughters and Sons of Reason. Thus We proclaim Our Carriers of Fire. Each realization of Our Will proceeds, revealing the fiery law of Hierarchy. Only the conscious adoption in life of the law of Hierarchy affirms the right path. Verily, space resounds with the affirmation of Hierarchy. Thus the wondrous life is being built. Thus the predestined enters into life. The Sons of Reason, the Daughters of

Light can make manifest the power of the higher laws only by obedience to the Hierarchy. Thus Our Hierarchs manifest Our power of Reason and Heart—thus unto Infinity!

83. Thus the Higher Reason creates upon Earth through the power of Hierarchy. Our creativeness requires the affirmation of Hierarchy in its entire scope, in its entire understanding, in its entire beauty. The understanding of Hierarchy reveals all possibilities. It is correct to view the law of Hierarchy as the summit of cosmic creativeness. Light pours from it, thoughts strive to it; thus one should direct the best strivings to the Summit of Hierarchy. Only when the highest affirmation enters consciously into life, can the highest be given. The fiery manifestation approaches!

84. How to affirm oneself in the Teaching? How to approach the higher law of Hierarchy? Only through refinement of thoughts and expansion of consciousness. How can one assimilate the Command from Above if there is no affirmation of correspondence? One should display receptivity to each energy. One should be able to adopt the vastness of the Teaching. Only correspondence can permit the saturation of the vessel. Therefore, the manifestation of breadth is worthy of a broad consciousness. On the way to Us one may attain only through Hierarchy.

85. All religions have introduced special movements and positions of the body that aid the accumulation of the energy and impel one to the Highest. When following Us, achievement may be arrived at through the saturation of one's heart, without fatiguing movements. He who succeeds through this means has an advantage, because the source of the heart is inexhaustible. The Image of the Lord, impressed upon the heart, will not grow dim and at any hour will be ready to help. This way of the heart is the most ancient, but it requires a considerable expansion of consciousness. One should not speak of the heart from the very first conversation, for then one may over-burden it aimlessly. It is likewise aimless to speak of love if the heart does not yet contain the Image of the Lord. But the hour strikes when one must indicate the power of the heart. I advise addressing oneself to the heart, not only because the Image of the Lord is already close but for cosmic reasons. It is easier to cross an abyss if the link with the Lord is strong.

86. Thus, it is not easy to be without the Lord. Repeat the Name of the Lord not only with the lips but rotate it in your heart, and He will not leave it—like a stone pressed into a crevice by the mountain waters. We say *Cor Regale* when the Lord of the Heart enters into the predestined chamber. One should shield oneself by the Lord.

87. The omnipresent Fire imbues each vital manifestation. The omnipresent Fire intensifies each action. The omnipresent Fire impels each striving, each undertaking. Therefore, how is it possible not to be imbued with the omnipresent Fire? The cosmic might, which underlies each impulse of man and each creative force, is directed to a conscious constructiveness. How carefully one should gather these identical energies for the construction of a better future! Only a conscious approach toward mastery of the power of co-measurement can manifest creativeness worthy of a better step. Therefore, each one on the way to Us must strive to creativeness, consciously directing his perceptions.

88. How greatly, then, must the disciple realize the power of perception and the comprehension that there exists only one law which governs the entire Cosmos—the Higher Will; along this line the evolution of the spirit is created. This law unites all related and manifested magnitudes. Striving toward fulfillment of the Higher Will leads to sensitiveness of perception. Only this path affords a decision in correspondence with realization and fulfillment of the Higher Will. Thus, We also offer Our creative striving to the Higher Will, and thus the arcs of consciousnesses blend in the One Flaming Heart. Yes, yes, yes! Thus the great cosmic step is created!

89. When your consciousness prompts you to the necessity of possessing the constant Image of the Lord, retire to a quiet place and direct your sight upon the chosen Image. But remember, one must decide irrevocably, because in case of treason the constant Image will be a constant reproach. After gazing intensely upon the Image, close your eyes and transmit it to the third eye. Exercising thus you will attain a vivid Image, and you will feel a special intensified tremor of the heart. Soon the Image of the Lord will remain inseparably with you. You can test yourself before the sun, and you will still see the Lord before you, sometimes without color, but afterward vividly and even in action. Your prayer will lose the need of words and only the tremor of the heart will suffuse your understanding. Thus one may reach in life much that is useful, but the consciousness must be in conformity with it.

90. One more useful exercise: Become accustomed to not being astonished or surprised at anything. But this should not be understood as the stifling of the spirit. On the contrary, in the complete readiness that gives birth to foresight, stand vigilant in the entire tremor of realization. Many wondrous things are approaching. One can understand them in accordance with one's own desire and one's own consciousness. But it is still easier to receive them through the Image of the Teacher. If you can visualize the Image of the Teacher in your consciousness with the most complete clarity you can transfer your consciousness into His, and thus act, as it were, through His Power. But for this, one must visualize the Image of the Teacher with utmost precision, even to the minutest detail, so that the Image may not falter, or suffer distortion, or change its outline, as frequently happens. But if, following the exercise of concentration, one succeeds in invoking a constant Image of the Teacher, through this one may gain the greatest benefit for oneself, for one's nearest ones, and for the work.

Such is Our warning when waves rise upon the ocean. I deem that the present time demands such concentration, because there is a vast success in the atmosphere; but success, like a magnet, also attracts unsuspected metallic fragments, and needles and nails may be poisonous. Understand this correctly. Do not be diverted from the conception of the Teacher. Do not be astonished or surprised, because it is good when one can disclose the next step of understanding.

91. If the clarity of the Image of the Teacher brings us into closest cooperation with him, then each clear and vivid conception of an object in our third eye makes it near and attainable. One of the conditions of ancient magic was to teach the vividness of objects evoked by our inner conception. If the object is called forth with all completeness of line and color, one can apply it for the most immediate reaction; one may, as it were, possess it. Without limitations of space, one can regulate and bring closer its possibilities; from the most customary objects to the far-off planets one can utilize this force. There is nothing of the supernatural in this; in a sense, the duplicate becomes identical with the original, and a vital connection thread is attached to it. One can gradually develop in oneself these abilities, upon habitual objects, noticing thereby that when a clear image is created, a peculiar tremulous vibration occurs, similar to a magnetic reaction. Thus, in studying the Infinite one can approach it by beginning with the most customary objects.

92. Likewise you will begin to notice that you see your own images as if in front of you. You must not wonder, because it is the increased development of the divisibility of the spirit. The projection of one's own image, and the sending of parts of one's spirit, impart to the developed third eye the image that is sent. One should know that simultaneously someone sees this image and receives help.

93. How important it is to guard the fiery impulse! Without this impelling force an undertaking cannot be saturated with the best possibilities. Forces applied to an undertaking are multiplied by the fire of impulse. Therefore striving is so necessary for increasing the forces given from the Primary Source. In all constructions harmony and co-measurement should be observed. Hence, for the saturation of Our undertakings one must co-measure what is given with the measures applied. The fire and the impulse sustain the life force in each inception. Without these the inception loses its vitality. Thus, let us strive to the confirmed fire bestowed by the Lord. Thus we can attain the fiery saturation.

94. As he embarked upon a ship, a purse of gold was stolen from a traveler. Everyone became excited, but the loser smiled and repeatedly said, "Who knows?" A storm occurred, and the ship was wrecked. And only our traveler was cast ashore. When the islanders called his salvation a miracle, he smiled again, saying,

"It is simply that I paid more than the others for my passage."

We never know when the good seeds sprout and how long the harvest of poisoned thoughts ripens. They also require time to ripen, therefore beware of poisonous thoughts; none will disappear without a trace. But where is that country, when is that hour when the ear of poison will ripen? Even though small but thorny, there will be no piece of bread which will not tear one's throat.

95. Is it possible not to harvest one's own sowing? Let the seed be good, or else poison will generate poison. Much can be avoided, but the treasury of thought will be the strongest. Thought, as the highest energy, is indissoluble and can be precipitated. Experiments with plants can prove the power of thought. Likewise, a scientist, if his thought is tensed, may take from the shelf just the needed book.

96. If We say, "Do not have desire," it does not mean to be insensate. On the contrary, replace desire with the irresistible command of a pure thought. In this command you invoke all the powers of Light, and you make their currents act in correlation with your pure striving.

Be, be, be joyous; not through desire, but through the striving of spirit. Be joyous; not through ancestral desires, but through the command of the entire consciousness, in order to create that luminous thread which unites all worlds. Be joyous; not because of the success of works already decayed, but in knowledge of the predestined and of that already inscribed in the scrolls of the future. Be joyous; not in the desire for repose, but because of the agitation of the elements, since only the agitation of the elements will serve you; for one cannot command the dead to revivify the living. Thus, understand that joy is a special wisdom, and do not abandon the fires of light above the crumbs of the feast.

That which is felt by the earthly senses is not significant; but let us apply the co-service of all the particles of Light. You await Me. You await the manifestation of help. But you do not know when help is needed and when the final hour of battle rings out. Yet, fixing upon Us your entire consciousness, aware that We shall not delay, you are building an indestructible bridge, and you are gathering the treasures of Might.

Perhaps the help is greatly needed. Let Us judge, because the time is ripe, and beyond the sea the pillars of Light already arise!

97. The fiery impulse gives life to the entire Cosmos. Each creative spark gives the impulse of motion to the striving of the spirit. How, then, not to affirm in each manifestation the fiery impulse that nurtures all tension and imbues each action? Therefore, one should develop the wondrous impulse of fire that gives life to everything. Thus the saturated fire can attract all corresponding energies. In the culture of thought, the fiery impulse should be developed above all. As the creative impulse assembles concordances, so thought attracts correspondences. Thus, guard the impulse of fire.

98. How wondrous are the sparks of spirit that manifest fire and striving! The fiery Service will bring to humanity so many signs of new evolution. Hence, Agni Yoga has so vitally entered life, and many signs regenerate and threaten our planet. One should accept all that is sent to humanity. Therefore the sensitive organism of the Mother of Agni Yoga responds to all Our sendings. Therefore the health should be guarded.

Verily, fires are raging! Much is attested, much is propelled, much is ahead!

99. The chief error of men is that they consider themselves to be outside of all that exists. From this issues a lack of cooperation. It is impossible to explain to the one who stands outside that he is responsible for what happens inside without him. The father of egoism has sown doubt and self-deception in order to sever the current with the treasury of Light. Nobody wants to consider that Light is the effect of thought, but the multitudes that inhabit the interplanetary spaces will willingly acknowledge the power of mental cooperation. They realize cooperation and understand responsibility. One can enroot oneself in a universal thought and thus acquire wings in heaven and on Earth—the foundation. Many valuable reminders about the link with far-off worlds are spread everywhere.

100. The spark of the spirit kindles the heart, hence Our Teaching is in need of spreading through the fire of the heart. How can one kindle the torches of spirit without the fire of the heart? Only fire uplifts creativeness and imbues each action. The energy that impels to the vital impulse must possess vital fire. Hence, in this law are contained creative powers. The tension of each energy calls to life the surrounding energies. Thus all materializations take place, gathering around them all energies. Therefore, the kernel of the spirit is a mighty accumulator.

101. How majestic is the law of Hierarchy! How constructive are all laws of Hierarchy! Verily, the ladder reaches Heaven. Thus, each one striving to Hierarchy can fulfill the Higher Will through a task given from Above. Thus, We build through Hierarchy; hence each Indication should be fulfilled as given by the Hierarch. Only thus can one fulfill the Higher Will.

Therefore one should truly guard the wish of the Hierarch. As pearls of the spirit one should guard the entire affirmed Source.

102. The self-sacrificing heart of an Agni Yogi contains the pain of the world, but it is a rare manifestation. As is said in a most ancient psalm, "I shall encompass within my heart the sorrow of the world. I shall incandesce the heart as the womb of Earth. I shall saturate it with lightnings. The new heart is the shield of the world. I shall inscribe upon it the sign of the Earth-Mother. The Cross of the Mother will be the sign of My fire." Thus knew the ancients.

And again a loyal heart is in the Service of the world. Therefore I say—health must be guarded. A vessel filled to the brim must be carried with caution.

One may rejoice at the kindling of the fire of the heart. Let us not forget how unexpectedly new fires are kindled.

103. Controversies are the carpet of the father of lies. The one who treads on it cannot see a man without maligning. The controversies in science usually stand upon the same carpet. It is amazing to what an extent people fill themselves with interpretations in which they do not believe. The contemporary churches are the best example of why the highest manifestation does not alter life. Therefore, let us protect the all-embracing heart.

104. For the evolution of the spirit the fusion of consciousness and heart is needed. When the forces are disunited, the spirit cannot act. Therefore striving for fusion of the subtle energies is so needed. In the entire cosmic constructiveness forces are in correlation, and by dissociation one can only suspend the preordained development. Therefore, the blended consciousness is being affirmed. Each force is in need of manifestation of a strained action, the more saturated, the more powerful. Hence, the fusion of the levers of heart and consciousness should be intensified.

105. The word that issues from the heart saturates space. Hence, thoughts that flow in an impetuous torrent form a sphere which becomes a defense against the poisonous gases of the planet. Thoughts become a defensive net for humanity. Only these luminous emanations give the strength to withstand the darkness. Hence it is so important to stratify space with words of the heart, they contain light. Thus humanity is uplifted upon the wings of thought. Thus evolution is being built.

106. What is the treasure of the heart? Not only benevolence, not only compassion, not only devotion to the Hierarchy but consonance with the Cosmic Consciousness when the heart, besides its own rhythm, even partakes in the cosmic rhythm. Such a heart can be trusted; it possesses straight-knowledge, it feels and knows, and as a manifested link with the Higher World it expresses the indisputable. The manifestation of the treasure of the heart is also very important for the formation of the subtle body. Try to imagine how important is the experiment with the subtle body. The densifying of the subtle body can give that of which the Teaching of Shambhala so sacredly speaks. One may have an unconquerable host, one may have irreplaceable co-workers, true, only temporary ones, but beyond the conditions of corporeal life.

107. The cosmic currents pass through the heart of an Agni Yogi. "The saturated heart senses all perturbations," thus the Ancient Wisdom speaks of the heart filled with Ether. That through which the Cosmic Space breathes, the sensitive heart breathes through also. That with which the Cosmic Heart breathes, the heart of an Agni Yogi breathes with also. Each vibration resounds upon the subtle strings of a sensitive heart, therefore one has to guard so greatly this cosmic treasure. The currents fill the heart and expand the sphere of its action; thus the cosmic correspondence is established.

108. Certainly, when wailing is borne through space, the saturated heart feels many reverberations. So great is the spatial battle and so tense are the waves of light! The Great Epoch approaches. How, then, not to overcome evil? Hence, the dark ones are so much on guard! When the great laws of Be-ness enter into life, how, then, shall the dark ones not be frightened? Thus I affirm Our Might!

Verily, it was rightly said about the significance of the fundamental principle of Our Work. Beauty has been proclaimed, therefore let us safeguard its foundation. Pearls must be guarded!

109. Why are the manifestations usually unexpected? There are two conditions—firstly, expectation always creates counteraction; even a conscious expectation can provide an energy superfluous for the manifestation. Secondly, in the case of an announcement, the black lodge may incidentally be informed. The presence of even one outsider can serve as an intermediary. The entire world is divided into black and white ones. Some serve consciously, others according to their nature, and the third present a jelly-like mass unfit for anything. The black lodge is strong, because for the combat with Light a powerful potentiality is needed. It is unwise to underestimate the forces of the adversaries, especially when their beloved Kali Yuga comes to its end. Certainly it is a decisive battle and one should take care that temptation and seduction do not touch the weak ones. The location of the main seat of the lodge of the dark ones was indicated long ago.

110. In former days black masses have been celebrated and statues to Baphomet have been erected. Now the dark ones have become more dangerous, because in trying to imitate Us they have eliminated many rituals and turned to the power of thought. The struggle against Us is difficult for them, but if the disciple's trend of thought is severed they can do harm. When I indicated to unite closely around the Lord, I advised the very urgent. Altogether, one should take My Indications as most urgent advice. It is time to understand that I give the Teaching not as a soporific, but for the saturation of the entire life.

111. When all the cosmic forces are strained, there can be no retreat without destruction. When the Forces of Light are grouped around the Light and the black ones around darkness, there is no retreat. Therefore, if the workers wish to conquer, they must gather as a mighty force around the focus. Yes, yes, yes! If an ordinary physical form is kept together merely by the cohesion of its particles, how much more powerful is the force emanating from the Hierarch! Hence, those who wish to conquer must adhere closely to the protecting Shield, to Hierarchy—only thus can one conquer. Only thus, during this threatening time of reorganization, can one live through the manifestation of turmoil. Thus, let us remember!

112. After having chosen the Lord and the Guru no retreat is possible. The path lies only onward, and sooner or later with ease or difficulties you will come to the Teacher. When the black ones surround you and close their circle, there will remain, only the path upward to the Lord. Then you will feel that the Lord is somewhere not far off and that the silver thread is above you. You have but to stretch out your hand! We can meet without the help of the black ones, but more often only he who is pressed from all sides reaches out to the silver thread, and only in distress does he learn the language of the heart. One should feel the Lord and the Guru in the heart.

113. They say, "We love and revere." But they remember it only like last winter's snow. Sleep is their lord! But the hour strikes, and the Lord will become their life and nurture. As lightning pierces the darkness, so bright will be the Image of the Lord. As a treasure they will guard each word from Above, for there will be no other way out for them. And few will be those who, having perceived Light, will be polluted by darkness. There is much of darkness around, and the path to the Lord is one. Remember about the Lord!

114. When the cosmic tension is so great, one should gather all strength for the defense of Light, because each uncertainty in Light gives access to darkness. Therefore, each foundation should be protected. When the forces are collected around Light, how can one not adhere to the Leading One? Only in this lies strength and victory. When the Cosmic Magnet is being shifted, certainly the course of Light must be followed, because only upon this crest of the wave can one swim over the manifested torrent. Thus the thought of Light will be like the Image of the Lord.

115. If people would only remember that they are always walking upon the edge of the precipice! For so it is. At any moment they may be carried off by a successful or unsuccessful change of course. Therefore, is it not possible to have in mind this link with the cosmic course, in order to look into the precipice without a tremor while hourly remembering its existence?

116. Certainly the sensitive organism of an

Agni Yogi contacts the cosmic current. Each wave is reflected upon the centers, and the receptivity of a sensitive Agni Yogi affirms the cosmic waves. That is why all cosmic and earthly waves contact the fiery centers in this way. Hence, the health must be so protected. Certainly it is difficult, but the cosmic consciousness is so wondrous.

Who will decide better and who knows better? Only the Hierarch. Therefore one has to guard every pearl. Thus, let them guard the treasures. Verily, I affirm that only thus can one conquer.

117. Earthquakes, volcanic eruptions, storms, fogs, shoaling, changes of climate, sicknesses, poverty, wars, revolts, heresy, treason—what other signs does humanity expect of the threatening time? Prophets are not needed, the most insignificant scribe may testify that never as yet have so many dreadful forerunners of Earth's disintegration been gathered. But deaf is the ear and obscured the vision. There has never been such an hour of disintegration as this planetary year! It is as if a path were being laid for the waves of fire, and the obsolete monsters of other days creep away unwilling to realize the price of that which takes place. Verily, the world is sustained by Magnets as imperceptible as the air and the flame of space, and just as indispensable as light. The Magnets sent by Us for Our manifestation are like the anchors of a ship tossed in the storm.

118. Thus one can see the end of Kali Yuga. It depends upon humanity where will be the beginning of Satya Yuga. We know that Satya Yuga is preordained, but its location and conditions may differ. My warriors, I can assemble you according to usefulness and devotion.

Man has fallen into a dark pit and closed the outlet with a black cover.

119. Thought controls the vital impulse. How, then, can one display so little of striving toward purification and development of thought? Consciousness attracts all vital expressions, and the creator of thought saturates space. Therefore it is so imperative to strive to broad thoughts and to the understanding of the foundations of Life. Each life is built upon its own orbit, and each life has a foundation upon which all actions must correspond to the Highest. Hence each thought must be directed to true achievement and must guard the highest striving. The quality of striving depends upon the impulse. Therefore one should develop all thoughts leading to the refinement of consciousness. Thus one can build a higher step.

120. Hence, when the highest striving toward the Lord is offered, the manifested orbit and focus should be guarded. Therefore, all Our Abutments should be protected, because clouds are all around. Victory is predestined, but all foundations should be protected, and the highest striving can bring all possibilities. The time is severe but wondrous. It is a time of consummation and construction. It is a time of highest tension and of earthly battle. It is a time which inscribes a great page and which is building a great future. Therefore the enemies rage, for the Highest Law enters into life.

121. Our Shield is one, therefore We value full realization. Partial glimpses are often extinguished. Hence one should be able to discern complete devotion. Only thus can one attain and broaden the consciousness. One should proceed by the higher path.

122. Chiefly, do not become dwarfs. For a dwarf even the threshold of a door is more difficult to overcome than a mountain. The thoughts of a dwarf will lead to shallow-mindedness and afterward to disintegration. It was correctly remarked that one should observe the influence of the basic aura. Those who have accepted it can cooperate, but its denial will be an actual sign of unfitness. One does not have to be persuaded about foundations; if they are not within the heart, nothing can explain them. Therefore, do not observe the motions of life as dwarfs. Likewise, the Teacher should not be adopted by the brain of subterranean dwarfs.

123. In Kurdistan there is a ruin called "the castle of errors." It is said that the castle was built by error, its location was chosen by error, the owner married by error, conducted wars by error, had councilors by error, gambled by error, fell ill by error, and perished by error. Only a certain amount of errors can be tolerated!

124. When various currents are gathering, measures should certainly be taken against them. Various currents are governed by counteractive measures. All hostile currents require bridling. Thus each arrow aimed at the Shield will be turned against the enemy. Thus the boomerang acts, and the currents of Our reactions will be powerful. Thus one must act, protecting all foundations and all the highest indications of the Hierarch. Verily, only thus can one attain.

125. Observe how people read the Teaching. Observe which passages they avoid and try not to notice. People especially often close their eyes to everything referring to betrayal and psychic murder. They do not even wish to consider that they can harm at a distance by their thoughts. Thus people avoid that in which they are most often guilty. One does not have to be a giant of thought in order to harm. Even a mediocre thought poisoned by the crystal of imperil will be very effective. To conceive treason means to accomplish an evident half of the whole, because an already poisoned shell will be receptive to the slightest impetus. Verily, poisoning by thoughts is even more harmful than narcotics. Likewise, one can remind about infection through thought-transmission. One may be weakened to such an extent that each infection can easily approach. Thought is like a key with which to open.

126. How can one avoid harm from the thoughts sent? Follow the one and same advice—intensify the striving toward the Lord. Along this direction one can acquire immunity. Therefore, I advise realizing Hierarchy from the highest spiritual striving to even the smallest bodily requirements; the silver thread is needed everywhere. Obstinacy and the black lodge will seek in every way to divert the thoughts from Hierarchy. Although subservience is highly developed among them, they keep it for themselves, knowing the immutability of this law.

127. The Spatial Fire dissolves all accumulations. But what a dam people build, and how they encumber space with non-understanding and a consciousness which so little comprehends the cosmic constructiveness! How can one create without acknowledging a Higher Leader? How can one build without sensing the thread that binds one with the Hierarch? How can one expect sendings when the spirit does not unfold to meet the Light? Only through adherence to Hierarchy and by fulfillment of the manifested Will can one be truly successful and attain everything that is affirmed. Yes, yes, yes!

128. Therefore each striving leading to the unification of the disciple with the Teacher leads to cognizance of the higher laws. The disciple in rejecting the Teacher acknowledges his own ignorance, because he arrests his development. Each force attracting the

spirit upward is a force of development. How shall we broaden our consciousness and uplift the spirit if we do not accept the Hand of a Hierarch? Conceit very harmfully retards progress! Hence it is urgent to point out to all those who speak against extreme devotion to the Teacher that only by the force of devotion can refinement of consciousness be achieved. The culture of the spirit and thought are to be followed, thus manifesting an unconquerable devotion to Hierarchy. Only thus is the spirit uplifted; only thus can one be affirmed in the evolution of the spirit. Hence, the beauty of Service is contained in the blending of consciousnesses. When the arcs of consciousnesses are blended, Light reigns, and the highest ordainment is affirmed. Only thus is the highest Law attained. Thus We create!

129. Let us write down questions for a disciple: "Dost thou not serve darkness? Art thou not a servitor of doubt? Art thou not a traitor? Art thou not a liar? Art thou not ribald? Art thou not a sluggard? Art thou not irritable? Hast thou a tendency to inconstancy? Art thou not negligent? Dost thou understand devotion? Art thou ready to labor? Wilt thou not be afraid of Light?" Thus ask disciples when preparing them for probation.

130. During construction one should develop all strivings toward synonymous understanding. Each task carries equivalent strength. One should strive toward finding this key. One cannot demand that a great manifestation be gauged by small measures. A small thought cannot be embellished. Small thoughts cannot make a hero. Only a subtle identity affords correspondence. Therefore the highest to the highest. The higher, the more affirming; only thus can one grow and introduce the predestined into life. The Highest Plan requires application of the highest measures.

131. Therefore, when We proclaim Hierarchy We are aware of the spatial battle which summons to the realization of the highest law. Creativeness requires the affirmation of the consciously accepted principle of Hierarchy. Thus We build, thus We summon to the subtle understanding of Hierarchy. Verily, the revealed Law enters life! Thus is affirmed the highest step.

132. I call attention to the saturation of the heart and the prayer of the heart for two reasons: firstly, it leads to a blending with the Higher World; secondly, it does not require a special time and can be performed during any labor. One may easily become used to a special sensation within the heart without fearing any ill effect. The heart will not be overtired by the Lord, on the contrary, only surrounding thoughts can ill-affect the heart. Thus, someday men shall finally realize the significance of thoughts, at least for the sake of their own hearts. Let them ponder upon the poison of sendings! It is time to pay attention to the amount of sicknesses generated by thoughts. During each sickness it is not bad to make a suggestion against negative thoughts. Magnetic passes over the affected organ can also be made. Nothing special is needed beyond a prayer of the heart, which creates a magnetic link with the Highest. During the laying on of hands one should not think of sickness, but should try to unite oneself with the Highest.

133. What benefit can be derived from small experiments and observations! Without wasting time, the disciple can pay attention to a multitude of small manifestations. Every day amidst your usual occupations pay attention to the various sensations of your organism. Each one in his own way reflects the cosmic manifestations, but one should fearlessly notice each sensation. Similarly one can even observe the life of the usual household objects under the influence of a definite hand. Repeat this to those who forget the impact of personality and contact.

134. The Cosmic Magnet attracts all energies that are shifted to a new center. Thus all outworn energies are shifted, yielding their place to the new ones. Therefore, at the change of forces all divided forces are lost in the cosmic process. Only Light and darkness are in opposition and are intensified in the cosmic conflict. Hence, striving should be saturated precisely with the fire of attraction, and one should seek Light against the black lodge with the entire impulse. It is necessary to shield oneself with devotion to, and realization of, Hierarchy and to dare against the darkness with all the levers of spirit and heart.

135. Thus each attempt of the dark ones will be a new possibility for Us and a boomerang for the adversaries. Only thus will the path be cleared, and each step of the enemy will turn into a trap for him. Thus We conquer. The time is great, the time is tense!

136. Only by the tension of all strength will you conquer. This must be remembered and applied. We have decided on complete success, it depends upon you to accept it. The entire garden of doubts, suspicions, fears, offenses, condemnations must be cast aside. If you desire to accept victory, every treason must be avoided, because the consequences of doubts and lack of respect for Hierarchy will disrupt all threads. When the ship is holding by only one anchor during the tempest, it is stupid to begin to change the chain. Guard the foundation, and ascend only through its growth. I shall be tireless in repeating about Hierarchy until you realize it. It is not enough to nod your head, it is time to think and to apply. I have reasons for repeating this.

137. The purple star is the sign of the highest tension, for tension and the continuous transmission of energy is the manifestation of co-creation.

Let no one take lightly My warning; when victory is weighed and defined, there can be no excuses or haphazardness. Remember, there is one Anchor, there is one Light! And when the greatest battle takes place, it is unforgivable to disturb the formation. I shall be very severe, because the time is at hand, and already some successes have been postponed. The burden is caused only by you. Guard the foundation! Many fires are introduced into action. Remember, the purple star indicates the highest tension.

138. Let us become accustomed to that which can be a true preparation for significant actions. Already, decisive dates approach each day. Wings are growing for the ascent that was already foretold in small coincidences as well as in decisive events. Again, the words of the Command shall be pronounced. It means that the fruits are again ripe. Again the dreams, the visions, and the hopes shall be gathered into a knot which will mark the next immutable step. Out of coincidences, imperceptibly minute, again are woven the tangible facts, and that which seemed unrealizable or postponed is again molded into a bonfire of events. Recall much that was told and apply it for the present day.

"I do not fear, for the enemies are serving, and our adversaries are bringing precious values into the treasury of the spirit." Thus, think benevolently, and aspire to the new step, to the new attainment.

139. The thread binding the Teacher with his disciple is the most powerful current and provides an evident defense. How, then, can one manifest one's striving without the Teacher? Those faint-hearted ones who say they will go alone do not know the significance of the protecting net. Hence, the non-acceptance of the Chain of Hierarchy gives a result equivalent to destroying the principle of construction. Thus, only with a powerful Hierarchy can one be affirmed in construction.

140. The sparks of causality fly in space, and each spark brings its effect. Thus, the non-acceptance of a Teacher leaves the disciple without guidance, and each action of such wandering spirits has no constructive importance. Thus, each spiritual striving must lead to the search for a Guide. Causality produces its wonderful sprouts when the disciple understands the significance of Hierarchy.

141. Certainly you do not doubt that I shall reiterate about Hierarchy. We shall insist, until We establish a firm understanding of this panacea. But each time We shall stress a new feature, for We do not repeat.

Someone may say, "I address myself with all my strength to the Lord, but it does not reach the Lord." Ask, "Was it sincere?" This quality of invocation is as necessary as Light. Each one may cast his eye into his heart and inspect the small corners of a decrepit world. Without sincerity there will be no current. Therefore strain all your forces and elect pure striving of the heart.

142. You often hear about the battle waged by the powers of darkness. Now you are in its very midst. Truly the Hierarchs themselves participate in the combat. The more glorious will be the victory. But hold My Hand as an anchor. I would not speak of the terrible danger without reason. Therefore, let us not lose the moment to unite, and, rejecting the past, let us strive into the future and hold fast in battle. It should be remembered that great is the honor of confronting the giants of evil. I know your tension, but accept it as a sacred ascent. Drive away all that is evil and dark.

Invoke Me often whenever the manifestations of Light are threatened. Remember Hierarchy!

143. When the intensified Magnet convokes all forces, each energy should be discriminated. Therefore, one should know which forces are admissible for construction and which can bring harm. Discrimination can be attained only through adherence to the Highest Consciousness, because only the scope of pure striving can reveal the affirmed Covenant of Service. Hence, one should learn to acknowledge all the higher laws, constructing life upon them.

144. Certainly, the cosmic manifestations reverberate against the feelings of a tensed Agni Yogi. Obviously the course of human deeds evokes subterranean storms and supermundane fires. Similarity is evidenced everywhere, and all that occurs has a like connection. Therefore, one should disclose a sacred feeling toward Hierarchy and the manifested heart. Hence, one should clearly comprehend the anchor of salvation and adhere to it with intense strength.

145. Unfortunately, the present time fully corresponds to the last period of Atlantis. The very same pseudoprophets and a pseudosavior; the same wars, the same treasons and spiritual barbarism. We take pride in the crumbs of civilization; the Atlanteans likewise knew how to fly across the planet in order to speedily cheat each other. The temples likewise became defiled, and science became a subject of speculation and dissension. The same occurred in construction, as if they did not dare to build solidly! Likewise, they rebelled against Hierarchy and were stifled with their own egoism. Likewise, they disturbed the equilibrium of the subterranean forces, and by mutual efforts a cataclysm was created.

146. When the link with the Lord is strong, mountains can be moved. Striving to Hierarchy creates that culture about which so much is spoken. Dead are those who presume that by means of earthly Maya they can create strongholds. It is as unwise as children dreaming to build a fortress out of mud! Only the world of spirit is truly strong, for it is indestructible and invincible. It may be pointed out that the first sign of culture is the absence of personal discords.

147. When the fate of the planet is being determined, the forces are distributed along the poles of Light and darkness; therefore, each spirit must guard itself from faint-heartedness. To side with Light means to walk with Us under the Banner of Hierarchy; to side with darkness means to walk under the yoke of the black banner. Thus, in time of battle one should fierily realize Our Might and build a lawful affirmation of life. Only thus can the challenge of the dark ones be accepted; for when the spirit is immune to faint-heartedness and treason, victory is manifested. Thus, let us be affirmed upon Hierarchy.

148. Certainly, when the battle proceeds, the creativeness of the forces is strained, and each loyal action adds a strong link to the chain of defense. Each heart manifesting devotion to Hierarchy serves as a smiting flame against the enemy. Therefore, only a pure striving to Hierarchy assures a right decision. Thus We conquer. True, when the battle is tense, there are many desiring to harm. Yet the plan is invulnerable, and only the evidence of complete striving to Hierarchy gives victory.

149. It was never said to rely upon the Lord. On the contrary, it was repeated, "Be imbued with the Lord!" There is a great difference between timid and inactive reliance and imbuing the entire being with the consciousness of the Lord. As an invincible sword, the consciousness identified with the Lord smites all obstacles! Doubt cannot find shelter where a flaming consciousness is kindled. There will be no fatigue where the inexhaustible Source of Forces is admitted. Fear cannot penetrate into the temple of invulnerable armor. Thus, I advise acceptance of My Shields, not through recourse to a saving protection, but by conquering through the blending of consciousness.

150. Attention should be paid to the kindling of the centers of the knees. Even spots upon the skin reveal the very same stigmata as does genuflection, which means that the prayer within the heart may be evidencing the same signs. Thus one may gather significant signs, for instance; the rhythm of cosmic energies in the heart or a strong swelling of the abdomen near these centers is attested, as are those of the larynx, the back of the neck, and the crown of the head.

I vouch for success if you are imbued with the Lord!

151. During a conflict of forces one should always observe the maximum of centralization. Therefore the power of the focus is so greatly needed, and each one in his turn must consider his position as bound with the center. Thus, the central power will emit all rays, and shadows will have to disappear. The radiation of the focus upon the spiritual plane is most invincible! Therefore immunity of the spirit can be attained through striving to the Spiritual Focus. Hierarchy is so wondrous in that it represents this mighty Focus. Therefore, one should strive limitlessly to the law of Hierarchy.

152. Thus the might of the Spiritual Focus is manifested by Us. Thus immutable are the laws of Hierarchy, and those who adhere to that affirmed might will find the right path. Hence it is so important to approach Us in the sole striving to fulfill the predestined. Thus victory is affirmed by Us. Therefore, one should gather all the best strivings to adhere to the Spiritual Focus.

The Focus radiates through the blending of consciousnesses. Our Focus is powerful through the blending of hearts. Our Focus is invincible, so I affirm! Thus, let the Spiritual Focus radiate in the heart of each co-worker. The creativeness of the spirit is inseverably linked with the corresponding striving. Hence, concordance is a lawful manifestation.

153. Dangerous is Maya when humanity thinks that it can create entirely identical objects. They forget that even the difference in the time of creation already effects a substantial difference. Thus, a standard can satisfy only an inferior consciousness. The mention of conventionalities of understanding corresponds to the understanding of Maya, but the foundations cannot be within the limits of Maya. Therefore, let us turn to the immutable, in other words, to the spirit's blending with Hierarchy. Having searched all corners of the planet we shall find the sole path upward. Thousands of hymns may be composed to this ascent, yet at its foundation will be the same identical striving of the spirit to the same spheres where its granulation takes place. One may study the idioms of all peoples, but nowhere will a word dare to express the immutable and unutterable Foundation of Be-ness and the path to the Father of all Existence. However, the heart in the hour of tension knows the Unutterable and feels the higher path.

154. In the dark the watchful voice of the watcher directs one to the Tower where the Lord holds his vigil. He who watches cannot carry out his service if he does not feel the Lord. And the world cataclysm is only the result of transgression against Hierarchy.

Transgression against Hierarchy means the shattering of all causality, all lawful effects.

155. The consciousness not blended with the Lord cannot strive to the law of accumulation in the Chalice. Only the power of the Cosmic Magnet can bring the spirit close to the Teacher. Verily, the one who adheres to the Higher Consciousness receives the power of thought. Only when a spirit accepts all transmissions from Above can he broaden his consciousness, otherwise the power concealed within the Chalice cannot be awakened. Thus, the thread of the bond is the ladder of spirit upon which the power of the spirit ascends. Creativeness is affirmed by way of this wondrous thread. Thus the ascent of the spirit proceeds through its bond with the Lord.

156. This bond unites Us and creates the best results. Thus, the most wondrous thread is the silver one uniting the heart of the Hierarch with his disciple. The light of the spirit is nurtured by this might. Therefore, when We speak of a united aura, We have in mind the actuality of the bond! Thus, the Counsels should be guarded as the Source of Light. Thus one can attract the best opportunities. Hence the sacred union of the Hierarch with the disciple is evidenced when the disciple's consciousness is striving toward the consciousness of the Hierarch. Thus a wondrous step is built by a blended heart!

157. You understand what each apostate inflicts upon the Teacher. If a special ray is assigned to each disciple, the severing of this thread must have a reaction. It is not without reason that the Teacher insistently questions the knocking ones, "Art thou not a traitor?" The severing of the thread between the Teacher and the disciple can be achieved only by a slow process, but impetuous betrayal is usually very painful to the

Teacher and to the traitor. Verily, the traitor's reason becomes obscured, and through the wound caused by the broken thread obsession occurs most easily. One should consider this process of betrayal as a physical danger, not to speak of the spiritual consequence. One should ponder how cautiously one must select disciples in order not to contribute to cosmic harm. Hence, each Teaching gives strong examples of betrayal. For betrayal there is no need to be precisely a Devadatta or a Judas. Even without these prototypes space is filled with fractured rays.

158. Without the bond with the Teacher one may give access to a dark dweller even by one pinprick of denial. Levity does not dwell far from betrayal. Thus one may imagine the consequences of the disciple's severing himself from the Teacher. It is time to pay attention to insane asylums and to verify the causes and conditions of such illnesses, especially now when this scourge is more dangerous than the plague.

Learn how to guard the thread with the Teacher and to fill the heart with the Lord. It must not be forgotten what is essential for an unswerving ascent. Neither works, nor circumstances, nor character, nor diverse reasons may erect barriers between the disciple and the Teacher. The manifestation of the Teacher signifies the initiation of the shortest path. To reject the Lord is to betray oneself.

159. One can see the unity of all manifestations when the spirit can reflect the best strivings. Space requires observations, and each manifestation is in need of conscious assimilation. Only when the foundations of creativeness are firm can one build for evolution.

Akbar used to say, "A cross-eyed person does not see the center." Thus, each vital action requires stability.

Before looking at two parallel lines, one should know which to choose. Hence stability is so indispensable, and only the closest approach to Hierarchy provides the correct path and the higher solution.

160. Thus, each disciple must approach Hierarchy and must affirm himself with the entire spirit on the closest approach. Striving to the Lord will give a full understanding of Hierarchy and will reveal to the spirit the silver thread. The center is occupied by Hierarchy. From the center emanate all rays. To the center converge all rays. Therefore, the stability of the spirit can attract positive manifestations. Thus, the power of blending lies in the heart. Verily, in the heart! Thus We create. Thus the higher step is affirmed.

161. Not only the direct link with the Lord but even an unconscious striving toward Hierarchy gives a glimpse of the communion with cosmic forces. Where colored sparks appear, the door is open to the chain of Benefaction. True, people seldom pay attention to obvious signs, however in merging into the life of the spirit one can not only understand the significance of these fires but may even perceive their interrelations. One may notice entire battles between the black and the blue sparks, and be convinced that the blue ones will always conquer the progeny of darkness.

162. The science closest to spirit is higher mathematics, if correctly understood. Thus abstraction becomes reality. The mist of knowledge can be illumined through Infinity. Certainly we must strive to all that can lead our consciousness beyond the boundaries of our planet. Only thus can the true values be understood. He who can understand synthesis will understand Hierarchy. One may reiterate much about Hierarchy, and We shall emulate the woodpecker until the knots of the bark are broken through. I repeat, if you do not understand Hierarchy in spirit, understand it at least for the benefit of your health. Manifest reverence.

163. Conformity between an action and the factor that called forth the action is powerfully evidenced in the entire Cosmos. All subterranean fires are called to the surface of the planet by the actions of humanity, which serve as a link between the worlds. Thus, the stifling gases call forth corresponding forces. Each human thought creates its own correspondences, hence it is impermissible to create without the action of the centers and attraction to the law of Hierarchy.

164. In cosmic creativeness everything is built upon succession, since the roots of each structure are held by the law of Hierarchy. Each task and plan is built in goal-fitness, and they are affirmed by the great plan of evolution. Thus, all Our affirmations bring beneficent manifestations. Only attraction to the Chain of Hierarchy can reveal the path to Infinity. Thus, the power of blending verily rules the world.

165. The physician who has an opportunity to study the sacred pains and does not do it is guilty. In studying those pains and comparing them with the actions that cause them, he could prepare the steps for the coming evolution. In reality, during the spiritual development of the world, sacred pains should not exist, but the surrounding imperfections create these pains. Thus, in comparing the conditions and causes, one can foresee the direction of evolution. Certainly, much can be improved in the human consciousness if we know that even earthquakes are called forth by the spirit of humanity. One can gradually gather many manifestations of which man is the creator. Thus, the sacred pains are the indicators of the next race in the clutches of the underdeveloped; hence, I say, Guard

your health. I say, Do not burden others by unnecessary sallies and irritation. The echo of errors resounds not only around you, but is carried along the entire Chain of Hierarchy. However, each caution is beneficial not only to you but it also strengthens space unto far-off spheres.

166. Verily, humanity is a link between the worlds. One should be used to that thought and try to apply it in life. It is strange that physicians do not avail themselves of the opportunity of becoming carriers of health, applying the knowledge of nerve centers, because precisely these centers are the spiritual antennae and magnets. Even a physical magnet is placed in a special vicinity in order that it may not lose its strength. Do not the nerve centers deserve similar attention? And must not people especially protect the representatives of the next race? The bridge between the shores is especially protected. One may demand of man, "Friend, do not evoke earthquakes."

167. The center that lights all beginnings of Our Works is based upon the law of Hierarchy. The impetuosity of creativeness is founded upon the center of Hierarchy. How obviously humanity deviates from the higher path and higher striving! He who is afraid of the manifestation of the Teacher will remain an ignoramus. He who rejects the Leading Hand will forever remain in error. He who is afraid to lose his individuality does not possess it. Thus one should ponder upon the great laws of Hierarchy.

168. There exists a misconception that the dark ones, being the antithesis of Light, are therefore unavoidable—this is erroneous. Darkness, the antithesis of Light, is nothing but unmanifested Chaos. The dark ones denigrate the manifestation of the combat of the creative Light against Chaos. It would be a sufficient task for humanity to make Chaos manifest and in that great battle to cooperate with the Great Spirits. But the dark ones have reduced the mastery of unbridled elements to the egoism of rebels and have begun to call forth Chaos instead of transmuting it into a working force. This crime is great, and the desire to extinguish Light cannot be considered an antithesis. The creative vanquishing of Chaos, or the "Dragon," is a constant achievement. But the battle with the dark ones is only a convulsion, impeding motion. The darkness of Chaos may be considered as a means for mental creativeness. However, the combat with the hierarchy of the dark ones is only a lost date, so needed for construction. Moreover, the dark ones constantly arouse mighty elements, not knowing, of course, how to master them.

169. It should be remembered that it is not the dark ones as such that are dangerous, but the forces evoked by them. Verily, one should compare great Light with great Darkness, but it is unfitting to consider as great those who build upon egoism. Thus, it is necessary to co-measure even in great manifestations. Certainly, let us not forget the harm sown by the dark ones who are like a brood of serpents! Even during battle with reptiles Hierarchy is needed, because everything disordered must be annihilated. Hence, let us remember where is great Darkness, and where the fierce enemy who seeks the annihilation of Light, having forgotten that without Light he cannot exist.

170. Construction requires intensified tension. Without this impulse it is impossible to build the steps of evolution. Each orbit is saturated with conscious striving, and each step requires its own affirming strength. Therefore, when creativeness assembles forces, identical energies are drawn to the focus.

Therefore, the more conscious the attitude toward the focus, the greater will be the action of correspondence and the more powerful the attraction. Cause and effect are predetermined, and the creative impulse is saturated by the fire of conscious striving. Thus the entire Cosmos is built.

171. Hence, when understanding is not founded upon Hierarchy, the manifestations of the focus cannot be so vitally displayed, and each one who isolates himself cannot find his way to Us. Thus, there are so many roaming shadows who cannot turn the affirmed key. Thus so many strivings are lost in space. Therefore, upon the blending of the arcs of consciousnesses, We build the future. Thus, Our fiery law ordains the blending of consciousnesses. Thus, one should be affirmed in the realization of the focus. The spirit can approach the realization of this fiery law. The manifestation of Hierarchy is the basis of constructiveness.

172. One more misconception: often, because of ignorance or self-justification, people think that their thought is insignificant and can reach nowhere, whereas the potentiality of thought is great, and for thought there exists neither space nor time. But those who think chaotically are, like those who wave their hands in the dark, unaware of the object they hit. Moreover, thought accumulates in space. One can conceive of a mighty choir of harmonious thoughts, but one can also imagine a flock of chattering black jackdaws. Such congregations also fill space and disturb the higher worlds. Dear thinkers, jackdaws, you are also responsible for the quality of your thoughts. Thus, even you create your future.

173. Therefore there is no way by which one can escape responsibility. Even the smallest thought enters into the megaphone of space and attracts to itself the same kind of locust, causing the smoky atmosphere of the planet. Thought can purify by destroying the microbes of disintegration, but it can likewise attract unbridled elements. Not without reason do the dark ones use especially underdeveloped people for certain machinations. You often utter the word cult-ur; it means the cult of Light. I remind you of how great is the common responsibility before Light if each thought can either obscure or purify space. Thus let us remember.

174. Certainly the path of Service can bring one to higher knowledge. Only ignorance could bring the planet to its present condition. Humanity has lost the understanding of the beauty of aspiration, and construction has been established upon the stupidity of isolationism. For this reason, unity of Service has been revealed as salvation for humanity. The entire power of constructiveness is based on Hierarchy. Thus the mighty thread unites the entire Cosmos. Verily, only in full realization of Great Service can the beauty of Spirit and the Might of Hierarchy be understood. Space summons to the fulfillment of the great Law. Yes, yes, yes! Thus the steps of true evolution are built.

175. Therefore, only a full understanding of Great Service can give disciples the aspiration to the Hierarchy. When the creativeness of the spirit can encompass Great Service, then all paths to Us are open. Therefore, striving to fulfill the Indications can be affirmed as an impulse leading to the highest Gates. Thus, let all the pearls of the Guru and the Tara be guarded. Thus one can fulfill all given possibilities. The time is pregnant and tense! Therefore, let the disciples strive to keep step with the rhythm of events; and consciousness should be strained in unison with all that occurs. Only thus does one conquer.

176. Verily, if you realize yourself as being constantly in the solemn presence of the Lord, you are already on the shortest path to Us. People loathe especially the routine of daily life; for them it is the symbol of weariness and descent, whereas for us the daily routine is perfectment and ascent; it opens the gates to Infinity. One can learn to love this daily routine, because it tempers the spirit and gives one courage to contemplate the endless chain of the ages of labor. For some, these ages are a menace, but a refined consciousness will accept them as the source of endless creativeness. Beautiful cults become dulled on account of daily routine, but how wondrous is the realization that daily devotion and a flaming love are offered to Hierarchy. If I shall say, "I love Thee, O Lord, and I am devoted to Thee, O Lord, and I reverence Thee, Teacher," by what a mighty choir will this song of praise be transformed on the far-off worlds! Thus, in each act of devotion one can open new locks; and how wondrous it is to feel the inexhaustibility of great concepts. The Ordainment can be concise: "Be aflame in heart and create in love!"

177. Learn not to count days and not to notice years, because there is no difference when you are in the great expanse of Service. One should learn to feel oneself beyond trivial usualness and to adhere in spirit to the manifested world of Beauty. Let us proceed together to where there are no boundaries or end, where one can transform each beneficent gleam into the radiation of a rainbow of blessing to the worlds.

Through devotion one can reach all gates. Let us not forget this even for a moment. Precisely, let us be filled with the smile of devotion, and let us bless the daily routine. Each breath of Ours contains a wondrous substance for the worlds in formation. Ponder upon the treasures which are given to us and which belong to the One who brought us a tear and a drop of sweat for our liberation. Let us also daily thank the Highest One.

178. How necessary it is for everyone not to disunite his heart and mind on the path to Us. Creativeness is affirmed by pure impulses, and it is most necessary to unite all the fiery centers. Thus, it must be realized that the matter of thought must serve as a link with higher substances, because only the subtlest thought can penetrate to them, and the refinement of consciousness can impel that force which controls mighty levers. Thus, only a united consciousness can fulfill the Higher Will. Thus the Chain of Hierarchy is affirmed. Thus a united consciousness rules the world. The Higher Will is transmitted to the closest spirit. Hence, the Will of the Hierarch must thus be fully executed. Therefore one must actively accept all that is given by a united consciousness.

179. The one who relies is dead, but the one who follows is alive. We did not promise to transport dead bodies, We vouched to lead courageous followers. One must ponder very attentively in order to discern the boundary between courageous following and faint-hearted reliance. Also, Our Indications must be understood without delay, for the sun shines differently at the morning hour and at noon. We should be accepted as daily nurture. And devotion will receive its answer if all forces are applied. Such must be the onward movement of those who follow the Lord. Our help, as you know, comes at the last hour, but the door should not be closed to Our messenger. Perhaps Our influence acts beyond the seas, nevertheless the striving toward Us must not be severed.

180. Disunion from the Guide stops the evolution of the spirit, because the disruption of the chain leads to isolation and impedes the creativeness of the spirit. Verily, only union with the Source of Light moves the spirit onward. Thus, striving to the Highest Hierarchy gives all possibilities and saturates the spirit with the power of Service. The orbits of Light are built by correspondence and by the power of fulfillment of the Higher Will. Thus is the path to Infinity built.

181. Hence it is most important to realize the significance of fulfillment of the Higher Will. Therefore, the power of blending is so greatly affirmed, for only in the blending of consciousnesses is creativeness contained. The disintegration of humanity is so vast because there is no balance. And the events on the planet indicate disunity with the Highest Consciousness. Thus, it can be confirmed that disciples must strive to the realization of Hierarchy. One can attain only through fulfillment of the Higher Will.

182. Gratitude is one of the main qualities of justice. Without justice one cannot reach the path of Great Service. Therefore, in pointing out the necessity for the realization of gratitude, We only assist the Great Service. How beautiful is gratitude! It so easily kindles the fire of the heart, and, as if in the presence of the Image of the Lord, it fills the spirit with nobility. The ingrate is, first of all, ignoble. We term nobility the benevolent accumulations from former lives, while upon Earth nobility is considered only according to one's birth. One should especially develop gratitude, because gratitude is the sister of loyalty. It is necessary to realize how difficult it is sometimes for the Teacher to combine the best possibilities. One must know how to assist by the fire of one's own heart.

183. The blended consciousness affords striving to the highest solution. Why, then, should such disunion take place when the entire Cosmos is affirmed upon the principle of blending? How can one be dissociated from the chain that holds the entire Cosmos? Lives must be built upon the principle of a tense cosmic chain. Only thus can Hierarchy establish the principle of fiery Service. Hence, on the way to Us one can attain only through Hierarchy.

184. Truly, divisibility of spirit is attained when the centers create flamingly. Thus the harmony of creativeness is imbued with this flame of the spirit. Each creative impulse kindles spiritual torches when it imbues space with its fire. Therefore the torches of the spirit can kindle auras. Thus the flaming centers kindle spiritual quests at a distance. Verily, great is creativeness. Yes, yes, yes!

185. The words that comprise the concept of Good are in great favor with Us. But one of them is utterly opposite to Our customs—that is comfort. Verily, investigate the history of humanity, and you will be convinced that nothing great was ever created in comfort. For a long time I have spoken repeatedly about the blessed obstacles, but there are few who love the struggle for achievement. However, it is inevitable to become used to the struggle, because otherwise it is impossible to temper the blade of the spirit. For earthly progress, as well as for the far-off worlds, obstacles and the ability to conquer them are needed. To be at rest does not befit a Hierarch.

186. Thus, We advise giving musk for strengthening activity, but We are definitely against narcotics which calm and deaden the intellect. How, then, will the quality of thoughts, so needed for the future life be developed if we dull it with poison? But medical science is lavish in producing living corpses.

187. It is correct to understand the eternal struggle, and to prepare one's consciousness as if to face an explosion, for only this will correspond to reality. My Hand will not tire in leading the combatants, but My Eye cannot tolerate the sight of lethargy in the intoxication of comfort. Having Infinity before one, yet not losing an hour and valuing the use of each minute —is Yogism. When the spirit naturally adheres to the Higher World and kindles a row of torches of the heart, one can call it a righteous path.

188. Spatial Fire is attracted to the earthly crust, and many subterranean manifestations fill the records of the planet. Certainly all events are tightly linked with humanity as well as with ensuing actions. Thus the manifestations evoked by the spirit of humanity create the Karma of the planet. How many of those perturbations are evoked by the spirit of humanity and the quality of thought! Therefore the coordination of the trend of thought with the created affirmations stratifies space which is saturated with the manifestations of Spatial Fire. Thus the life of the planet is forged, and the striving of humanity must be directed to the purification of space.

189. Thus, thought can be commanded to direct itself to a benevolent intention. Humanity dreams of a better future, still it does not know how to pierce the depths of darkness, because the basis manifested by the Cosmic Fire is not observed in life. The laws of gravitation have lost their significance, hence only the law of purification can provide that which the planet has lost. Verily, only purification can provide the essentials for efflorescence. The key is within the spirit, and only this key can vouchsafe achievement. Hence, on the way to Us, the entire beauty of spirit must be understood.

190. It is necessary to understand it literally when I say that a considerable number of sicknesses should be treated with psychic energy. Infection of the nerve substance will always be the primary cause of various diseases. In the infection of the nerve substance the Higher World unites with the lower; through a gap in the nerve substance any intruder can penetrate, beginning with obsession and ending with cancer. Yet the nerve substance can be protected only by psychic energy. This training of psychic energy will be the true prophylaxis of humanity. At least a pure thought can be applied, thereby protecting the entrances to the nerve spheres. Even such a simple measure will be useful. Also, psychic energy will be the best purification during the period of a hidden disease. But terrible is the decomposition of the nerve substance under the influence of drunkenness and all kinds of vices. Ponder upon the state of the subtle body, when the subtlest nerves assume the significance of a skeleton! Bones belong to Earth, nerves to the Subtle World, Light to the Spirit.

191. But again I shall turn to Hierarchy. Nothing can so greatly strengthen the nerve substance as the Chain of Hierarchy. But how to strengthen man in the importance of accepting Hierarchy? Even those who hear about it do not accept it as a vital condition, and thus harm themselves and the great Plan. The harm inflicted upon Hierarchy has no equivalent and cannot be expunged. I cannot even call it an error. It is already apostasy—not levity, but treason.

192. Striving toward constant abiding with Hierarchy can provide the necessary steps. How can a tree stand powerfully if one tries to uproot it? Only contact with the pure current gives balance to the forces. Hence, only the roots of Hierarchy can uphold a structure. Each digression brings harm to the mighty growth. One should be consciously affirmed in the understanding of the Power of Hierarchy. Through

the clefts caused by disrespect to the Hierarchy, black forces creep in. Hence, one must understand unity with the power expressed by the Higher Might. Thus can one attain.

193. He who strives upward without Hierarchy may be compared to an archer who shoots arrows heavenward with closed eyes, expecting that one of the arrows will reach a bird. All chance must be eradicated from life. We know in which direction we move, and we trust our Leader—only thus will no arrows be aimlessly lost; and the Leader knows how to guard against poisonous sendings. However, let us reverence the Leader not only in words but within our heart, and He will grow, together with us; because in approaching the great we grow, but diminution is unavoidable with retreat. This law can easily be represented graphically. Let us imagine how out of the seed of the spirit two diverging lines proceed toward Light into Infinity and how each right move verily magnifies us.

194. Constant contact with the Higher Reason draws the spirit to higher cognizance. Constant application of higher laws brings the spirit to the orbit of the Cosmic Magnet. Invincible is the path that is built by the Command of the Higher Will. The Power of Hierarchy is the Might saturated with the fire of creativeness. Submission to the Power of Hierarchy means the offering of fire to the General Good. How dimly this concept burns in human understanding! The consciousness that does not absorb this understanding can only mumble the great words, being incapable of applying them to life, because only a heart saturated with the greatness of Hierarchy can understand the entire majesty of the cosmic law. Thus, the attraction to the Magnet can take place only through the realization of Hierarchy.

195. The Chain of Hierarchy lawfully leads world-construction. Verily, the creation of subtle bodies can be affirmed only by the subtle matter of thought. The weaver of his own body does not suspect what he introduces into the web of his body by severing himself from the Highest. Therefore let us ponder upon the most vital—the Chain of Hierarchy.

196. You may be asked how the entrance upon the path of Service is defined. Certainly the first sign will be renunciation of the past and full striving to the future. The second sign will be the realization of the Teacher within one's heart, not because it is necessary thus, but because it is impossible otherwise. The third sign will be the rejection of fear, for being armed by the Lord one is invulnerable. The fourth will be non-condemnation, because he who strives into the future has no time to occupy himself with the refuse of yesterday. The fifth will be the filling of the entire time with labor for the future. The sixth will be the joy of Service and completely offering oneself for the good of the world. The seventh will be spiritual striving to the far-off worlds as a predestined path. According to these signs you will discern a spirit ready and manifested for Service. He will understand where to raise the sword for the Lord, and his word will be from within his heart.

197. Do not strive to only a customary decision. One may subjugate many heads by customary speech. But this speech will be unintelligible to the higher worlds. Earthly prosiness sounds like the barking of a dog. No magnet will attract such a husk, and fire cannot burn without oil. But let us discriminate between commonplaceness and daily labor, because many people seek contradiction where it does not exist. Notice such people; they are not successful, because their thought is with yesterday. Let us not be bound by anything of the past. Also do not look for friends according to yesterday, and know at once how to test their hearts.

198. With the growth of assimilation grows the feeling of responsibility. Facing the Great Plan, understanding of responsibility must be made manifest, therefore with each decision the full feeling of responsibility should be realized. Complete responsibility imbues one like Spatial Fire. Full responsibility must imbue each action; for the feeling of containment can only be affirmed when the sense of responsibility impels the spirit to the fulfillment of the Will of Hierarchy. Hence cosmic daring suffuses the Carrier of Fire. Therefore the affirmation of the Higher Will can be realized when the spirit is truly filled with responsibility. Thus, victories are achieved. Thus, those are invincible who fulfill the Will of Hierarchy.

199. The fiery Envoy of the Hierarchy acts as a mighty fiery Will. The Hand of a Hierarch directs as a Higher Hand. The Hierarch saturates as a propelled magnet, hence one must act consciously. Thus, the spirit striving to the realization of the Teacher can be affirmed on the path, but the spirit rejecting the concept of the Teacher may betray the Hierarchy.

200. Thus, one should fulfill all that is preordained, applying an understanding of the best date. Thus, one should remember how greatly the design of grains of sand is changed under the strokes of different fingers. Even the fingers of one and the same hand produce different designs to one melody; still more diverse is the rhythm of different people, but a fiery heart perceives the subtle differences in rhythm. Straight-knowledge is the kindled fire of the heart. It is difficult to express in words when this string of the heart will resound, but Hierarchy can point out this hour of transfiguration.

201. When the world is convulsed, the sign of Maitreya is given as an antidote. When the foundation of Our Works was laid, the forces of the spirit were strengthened. Thus the sign of Maitreya has been affirmed. And in Our Day, when the manifestation is affirmed, one can repeat, How vitally the power of the spirit has entered into life and how greatly this new power has been affirmed in consciousness. Hence, the consciousness must be applied to a mighty understanding of Hierarchy, which holds the chain of all strivings. Thus, each manifestation of beauty placed by Us in the foundation of Our Works must be acknowledged as a vital action. Thus the power of the foundation consists in beauty, and striving to the fulfillment of the Higher Will, will lead to the predestined victory. Thus Our Towers should be built, verily, in beauty!

202. It is premised that around good deeds difficulties always arise. What does this prove? Does it prove the weakness of Light and the power of darkness? Let us remember, however, that with developed vision many things are perceived. Similarly, a refined spirit perceives much that is inaccessible to deadened senses. Besides, are we not in need of a counteracting force in order to become accustomed to withstanding the unmanifested elements? This benevolent force of resistance is apprehended only in action and is accumulated as an armor of the spirit. Can one complain about the development of resistance to evil? No, certainly not—this armor of the spirit is not only a defense it is also a magnet which attracts allies. Therefore, bless everything that develops counteraction and resistance to evil.

203. You may meet people hastening with their attainments, and they may think that We are slow. But lead them under the night sky and point out the radiance of the countless worlds. Say, The Lord leads you toward this creativeness. Is it possible to be slow on this great path? We must prepare ourselves to be co-creators. It is necessary to preserve and multiply the seeds of consciousness, because the entire world is sustained by the power of consciousness. There is no power to withstand a consciousness purified of egoism. One can prepare oneself to cross all bridges with a fiery consciousness which is atremor with the pulse of Cosmos, and which, in the seed of its spirit, responds to all tremors of Earth and knows the truth of the peoples. One can apply all sacred powers of the heart to becoming co-creators of the flaming Logoi by conquering death. But so long as such daring is not instilled in the heart, the consciousness cannot grow infinitely in this direction. We call it *Via Regale*. Therefore, Fiat Rex is where the spirit, reverencing Hierarchy, dares!

204. Into the base of an affirmed orbit there is always set a single will, which binds all manifestations. Therefore, the focus is the radiating source that imbues all with fiery creativeness. Beautiful is the will that imbues with creativeness and impels each energy of the spirit into the higher spheres. Hence, the orbit that is built by the manifested will is expanded by the Spatial Fire through assimilation of the saturated fires and by its correlation with higher spheres. Thus, a great thought brings the spirit to great attraction, and the Will that radiates the highest fire attracts the spirit into the highest orbit. Thus, wondrous is it to be attuned with the Higher Will. Verily, only thus are revealed the orbits of the Infinite.

205. Therefore the powers of the Cosmos are so affirmed in space. Each center feels each vibration; therefore, during the changing currents the fiery centers are so sensitive. Therefore, the health must be guarded.

206. The experiment with the densified astral body, in substance, is not an attempt, but a plan-fitting inception of the Sixth Race. It should not be thought that a densified astral body will remain unstable for a long time. The preparation that can sufficiently densify it has already been found. Thus, amidst the earthly turmoil We assemble a new race. Certainly, means have to be found which will purify the lowest strata of the earthly atmosphere. But already there are some possibilities. The emulsion given to you pertains to the remedies for purification, destroying poisons through the pure film of the skin.

207. Let us not think that the next race will fall from heaven on rosy wings. No, here also one cannot dispense with a laboratory. We welcome it if now thoughts about the transformation of the race are strengthened. For this, we shall not resort to the help of monkeys, but shall turn to the foundations of human nature and add the accumulations of the vegetable and mineral kingdoms. Thus the human spirit will receive a regenerated garment. Precisely, man can and must think of the future, not with prejudices, but starting from the facts of the existence of bodies of different degrees. If such degrees exist, then no one can maintain that intermediate stages based upon mutual advantage may not be found. It is difficult to understand Hierarchy if its continuity is not comprehended. Similarly, the various degrees of bodies exist when they are mutually nourished.

208. You can understand how the black lodges oppose humanity's perfectment, how they prefer the fate of Atlantis to the light of a new body. Let us be on watch, let us be vigilant, let us follow the Lord!

209. The affirmation of the Teacher intensifies all creative forces. Without the Teacher there can be no link in the great chain of creativeness. Hence all the forces of Cosmos which manifest the course of evolution can be affirmed on the principle of Hierarchy. How can one build without the focus of attraction? Each force has its own tensions, which call forth creative strivings from the source of cosmic fires that gathers Light and spreads Fire around itself. Verily, thus is the Cosmic Focus affirmed, and life must be built around a focus. Creativeness is limitless!

210. Therefore, only through broad realization of the focus can the best manifestation be attained. When we cognize the affirmation of Hierarchy, then each action has its focus. Hence the realization of the focus is so important. The hand that hesitates after realizing the focus is in need of strengthening. Thus, let the consciousness expand in the direction of the focus. Thus the Guru and the Tara have brought the entire creative fire.

211. Thought is the basis of creativeness. It can be visible and measured. One has to regard thought as the creation of independent action. From this understanding issues a correct attitude toward the consequences of thought. It is often asked why We do not cut off the consequences of a thought. But thought is a newborn entity of the spiritual plane. Notice, thought is not an abstraction, not a substance, but an entity with all the signs of a self-sufficient existence. As an entity of the spiritual plane, thought cannot be annihilated. It can be opposed by a similar entity of greater potentiality. In this lies the essence of Tactica Adversa, when a monster is permitted to attain its complete ugliness in order that afterward it may be destroyed by a ray of Light. Hierarchy will be the best pledge of the true might of Light.

212. Call Hierarchy your touchstone, upon which you can test the efficiency of quality; for if you do not admit the existence of the best and the most luminous, then there is no need to safeguard and perfect your own Monad. The existence of Hierarchy is the foundation of the entire life. Remember that Hierarchy acts through the legion of Service. Do not delay in assembling these legions, for there is no task more successful than Service to Hierarchy.

213. Power directed for the General Good is always multiplied in space, and there results a link with the higher spheres. But that force which emanates from evil becomes a boomerang. The formation of affirmed emanations gives power for the saturation of space. The manifestation of evil arrows tenses the lowest strata, which become densified to such an extent that a rebounding blow is inevitable. Thus, each thought that is attracted to Light draws after it a bright radiation, but an infected arrow can pierce the crown of the sender's head. There are many such manifestations pointed out upon the spiritual plane. Hence, space must be guarded against infection, and the quality of thought must be kept high. Thus, one may manifest conscious cooperation.

214. Certainly, when the black lodge directs its arrows against the White Brotherhood, the consequences are self-destructive, and the manifestation of a rebounding blow is unavoidable. What you heard is a consequence of self-destruction, because the aimed arrow returned to the sender. Hence, let each one be affirmed in the understanding of Our Power. Nothing can touch the one who evidences a full faith in Our Might and in the Hierarchy. Our Rays are always on watch and Our Hand is indefatigable. Thus the full Might of Hierarchy must be understood.

215. Thought is a spatial entity. Much attention is given to thought-forms, but, except superficially, little acknowledgment is given to the effect of thought, whereas it is precisely the consequences of thought that most seriously strike the surroundings with their effect. Sound reacts upon the most unexpected objects. The reaction of thought is just as subtle. He who indulges in self-pity may lose money, or if he is wrathful, he may be subjected to serious incrimination. Thus, various are the effects of wandering thoughts. One should remember that no thought can remain without consequences. It may affect a person who is far away, but in this person the ball of fate will find its generator. Certainly there can be no accident in this, yet the design of the flight of thought is so complex! The consequences of thought should be observed as much as possible.

216. All physical tension should be eliminated, for one cannot play the violin with a broom. Also, laughter causes disturbance of the closest strata of the atmosphere. When the heart is aflame, it resounds like a bell upon the far-off distance. It is rare to hear a Yogi laugh boisterously, for his joy is not in loud laughter, but in the saturation of the heart. Precisely, "joy is a special wisdom" not only in its essence but also in its exterior.

217. One of the mighty qualities of spirit is steadfastness. How can one develop and expand one's consciousness when steadfastness is lacking? How else can one verify intentions and actions if there exists no such mighty impulse as steadfastness? For each one on the path there is but one immutable Might—Hierarchy. Upon this sacred Principle one may construct; from this sacred Summit one may contemplate the world;

upon this Stronghold the spirit becomes winged; upon this Summit can be built a mighty evolution. Therefore, when the spirit tries to create an illusory world of selfhood, it is certainly difficult to advance. Thus, in limitless creativeness there is the beacon fire—Hierarchy. Thus, by steadfastness in Service one can broaden one's consciousness and encompass the law of Fiery Hierarchy.

218. Hence, one must remember that disparagement of Hierarchy is treason; that indifference toward Hierarchy is treason; that a negligent attitude toward all that pertains to Hierarchy is treason. Thus, We affirm that responsibility must be realized for each spoken word, for each deed and each action.

How can one not be affirmed in a fiery transport to Hierarchy when the most sacred fire is Hierarchy! Therefore, let each one ponder on how better to serve Hierarchy, eliminating all evidences of selfhood, disparagement, levity, and the standardized formulas of the crowd. One should cooperate more fittingly, consciously accepting the Fiery Hierarchy.

219. The language of the subtle body is expressed through the saturation of the Brahmarandhra center; other than this, there is no need to strain oneself in pronouncing all letters. The sound of the first letter is sufficient, because the rest is understood by the heart. Likewise, the music of the spheres does not require melody, but is based upon rhythm, for the rest resounds in the heart. Precisely the heart is the link between the worlds, and only the heart can respond to the heart of the Lord and to the entire Hierarchy. One may be bereft of sight and hearing, but the heart will be the best substitute, and even a more subtle expresser of the essence.

220. During cosmic perturbations the spirit verily

begins to ponder over the pages of Be-ness. When fear overcomes the spirit, every constructive will is paralyzed, and construction is stopped. The more powerfully must that spirit build which knows that a fiery striving leads it to mighty knowledge of the Cosmic Magnet. Therefore, those who follow Hierarchy must be rid of fear, for the heart that contains the greatness of the Plan is invincible; and under the fiery Shield of the powerful Hierarchy the great future is being built. Hence, amidst all cosmic perturbations and vital changes there is but one anchor—Hierarchy. In it is verily salvation!

221. When We assert that Hierarchy is the Shield, it means that upon it is based the principle of the fundamentals of creativeness of the saturated fire. Therefore, We have revealed to the world the Carriers of Fires, and have given the manifestation of Beauty. Therefore, let the disciples spiritually uphold that principle which is life itself. The spiritualized Source which imbues all works must be affirmed in the heart and consciousness.

222. Unusualness is a happy quality of each decision. Let us take the instance of an illness. The physician may give his best diagnoses and all his medicines, but this usual way may not lead to improvement. But a Yogi gives advice, and this unusual decision creates a strengthening condition. The medicine of a Yogi is not from an apothecary and avoids narcotics, but it contains the secretions of glands which, like food, strengthen the substance of the nerves. The same property is possessed by the secretions of trees, the resins of which can carry through the pores of the skin the same fortification for the nearest nerves. Certainly, purified resin can be taken internally. The best purification will be through the solar ray, but this requires a long time, because the process of sedimentation is very slow. Each oil may be purified just as slowly, but this purification is not to be compared with any chemical process. Thus the unusualness of the Yogi's advice has an advantage over the usualness of that of physicians. Thus act.

223. All events collect around one focus. All signs point to the one focus. One manifested fire exists in everything, the seed of which attracts all corresponding energies. Thus all cosmic events are fulfilled. Hence, only a full realization of the one focus can direct the spiritual quests to the affirmed seed. The immutability of creativeness enters vitally when the focus is realized. For thus, verily, striving enters into the channel of action! Therefore, only in this way can we attain steadfastness of spirit. Thus can one be imbued with a subtle realization of Infinity.

224. Hence, so beautiful are the strivings to the single focus of Hierarchy. Only thus can one assimilate all the Commands of the Highest Forces. Only thus can one approach Our Ordainments and adhere to fiery creativeness. The fiery focus, all-illuminating, all-containing, gives life to each creative inception. Therefore it is so important to comprehend Hierarchy. Yes, yes, yes!

225. Pay attention to a special characteristic of all animals and birds that exude secretions similar to musk. The furs and feathers contain an oily substance, as well as heat, as if a kind of resin or mountain oil had saturated them. The plumage of the birds takes on a metallic hue, as a result of their feeding upon roots and grains that contain much psychic energy of the vegetable kingdom, in other words, of resin. Minerals also give out psychic energy through the vegetable kingdom or through the air, where the Fire of Space

has the same properties as thought manifested by the spirit. One can now understand the ancient comparison that termed thought a flame. What remarkable experiments could be performed by linking a chain of reactions of the psychic energy from minerals to the subtle body! One could observe how varied would be the reactions of the furs and feathers of certain birds and animals. Is it casual that in the ancient palaces and temples metallic peacocks were kept? One may ponder why musk animals and monal birds breed at almost equal altitudes. Are there not the same soils on the heights as in the plains? When we shall purify the atmosphere of the plains we shall have to pay attention to the depths of Earth, invoking their psychic energy.

226. The foci of life should be gathered. Thus is accumulated that quality which is called culture. Culture cannot be created instantaneously. Nor can the foci of life make their appearance like cannon balls. Thus, the manifestations of life demand tuning like the instruments of an orchestra. It would seem that I speak of various subjects, yet they are all nothing but Fire, Energy, Hierarchy!

227. The vitality of all origins is affirmed by the fiery principle of Hierarchy. Only the principle of the Highest Hierarchy affords balance and striving to each affirmation. Therefore, in establishing cosmic principles the main impulse is the Chain of Hierarchy. The creativeness of humanity depends upon these affirmations, and only adherence to the Highest Chain affords the necessary force. Thus, each chain is a link of a greater chain, and the might of this Chain reigns in Cosmos. Hence evolution intensifies each smaller chain, linking it to the great, limitless Chain of Hierarchy. Thus the Might of the fiery Hierarchy soars high. Yes, yes, yes!

228. How, then, can one be affirmed in the Chain of Hierarchy? Only through the heart and endless striving toward Service, only by complete assimilation of the Plan of the Lords and through creativeness of the spirit. Thus, verily, each one on the path must accept the Service of the heart. Thus the immutability of the Chain of Hierarchy is verily affirmed.

229. Origen reasoned, "Does Bliss emanate or is it sent?" Being aware that Bliss is an absolutely real substance of the highest psychic energy, one can understand that this reasoning had a sound basis. Thus, heat emanates from light, but a burning glass is needed to produce fire. Psychic energy certainly emanates from each organism that possesses it, but in order to receive a direct result one must gather and focus it consciously. This consciousness is like a burning glass. It is necessary to discriminate between an unconscious flow of psychic energy and a sharpened arrow of precise consciousness. If even the highest energy does not reach the goal when sent unconsciously, then how greatly in need of a focus is human energy! Destroy the focus and the fire will not be manifested. Without fire, darkness and cold await us. Let us remember how the vivifying heat and Light can reach us.

230. One should learn to value the warmth and light of the focus, and remember that the rays of the One Light emanate from one direction. Let us compare our position to a physical law and we shall see the sole foundation for success which is unshaken. What is success if not the effect of the correct application of a law? Thus one must learn to sense the channel of Hierarchy.

Thus, often will he be held responsible who did not know how to rule, because weakness is not a justification. Where there is a burning glass there is also fire, for it is not difficult to wait for the ray of the sun. We have been waiting for centuries; it is less difficult to wait for days. Remember often that Bliss is above you and not beneath your sole!

231. When space is saturated with fires, each cluster scintillates in the centers; therefore, a sensitive organism feels all approaches, and each change of cosmic currents is reflected upon the centers. The affirmation of consonance acts upon the centers, and each vibration reflects on a particular center. Likewise, each planetary event is reflected; and during revolutions and shiftings a sensitive organism resounds to each affirmation. Science will take up the question of consonance, and it will be possible to determine exactly the action of intuition in accordance with the sensations of the centers. Only by such investigation of consonances will it be possible to determine the cause and cooperation. Hence, the study of consonances is the science of the future.

Thus, when the centers vibrate it means that the Spatial Fire is raging. The energies propelled to the subterranean fire rush forward powerfully. The cosmic consonance intensifies all resounding centers; therefore, it is so important to carefully guard the health and the resounding centers.

232. Even the best friends test each other with some ingenious move at chess or through a dangerous hunt. Even in a besieged fortress the army carries on maneuvers in order that the hands of its members may not grow stiff. And those defeated are not offended, nor do the conquerors boast, since it is only an exercise in resourcefulness.

I remember how once "The Light of the Eyes," Jehangir, came running and complaining that his playmate, Jeladin, had pushed him severely. We asked, "How did it happen?" "Jehangir was a hunter and Jeladin the tiger." I said, "It would be amazing if a tiger were to be transformed into a dove. Thank thy comrade, who gave thee the imitation of the fury of a beast. Tomorrow we shall go to hunt real tigers; be resourceful with them. But remember that a ruler never complains." Thus it happened during the time of Akbar, the unifier of India.

We must firmly remember to what the understanding of Hierarchy obligates us. One can see how useful are tests, otherwise the light that is kindled only in battle will grow dim. The light of battle and daring is the most precious.

233. It is necessary to become as accustomed to battle as to daily labor. One should understand a battle not only as a test of excelling in strength but also as a source for the accumulation of energy. We cannot think of mastering the elements without a battle. And how ready must we be at a call, for otherwise we may waste the action of the Higher Forces. Hierarchy does not mean the steadfastness of repose, but steadfastness in the midst of battle. Can something else be substituted for battle, when Our Magnet is tense and each victory is the joy of the entire Hierarchy? If it is difficult for some to accept Hierarchy through love, let them accept it as a fundamental necessity.

234. All nations knew about Guardian Angels and have preserved these traditions for millenniums. All Teachings knew about the Mighty Protectors of humanity who guided nations. Why, then, has our time denied the Highest Leaders? When has the world existed without Protectors? And how can humanity be affirmed by the concept of the absence of a Leader? The basic principles of Be-ness are intensified by the laws manifested by the Leaders; and the cosmic laws do not change, but grow with cosmic affirmation. Therefore, the Protectors of humanity and the almighty Goddess Fortuna create humanity's destiny. The realization of this great law can impel humanity toward the Chain of Hierarchy.

235. Hence, each spirit must understand the Hierarchy as Protectors of humanity. Thus evolution is built, and creativeness is fierily affirmed. Thus the law is affirmed; only thus is life suffused by the great might of unity. Thus is life created.

236. It is correct to investigate the importance of vitamins, but one should also experiment with the reaction of psychic energy. One can see that a conscious consumption of vitamins manifoldly increases their usefulness. Likewise, it can be observed that the absorption of vitamins while one is irritated may increase imperil, since an unconscious energy is strengthened at a point where consciousness is gathered. One can understand why the partaking of food was considered sacred by the ancients. It is easy to understand to what an extent realization multiplies all energies. So many simple experiments can be performed with a minimum of observation. In order to increase respect for consciousness one may call energy Atma, or psyche, or life, or consider it sacred, but it is necessary to study its significance. By this channel we approach Fohat, or atomic energy. It is essential to observe the microcosm and transfer the formula to the Infinite.

237. It is necessary to find a few Western scientists who could free themselves from prejudices and begin to investigate the conditions of psychic energy. Certainly, the heights of the Himalayas will provide the best possibilities for scientific research.

238. How powerfully is cosmic energy reflected

in the human organism! Each cosmic fire meets consonance in the human organism. How much can be learned through a spiritual approach to the investigation of all manifestations of the centers! If one were to consider the human organism as the reflection of the manifestations of Cosmos, many consonances could be perceived; and the centers would become a fiery manifestation for science. Only a spiritual approach will reveal the significance of all cosmic correspondences and their human reflections. The centers may be regarded as accumulators of cosmic energies. It is correct to think about direct nourishment for the highest centers. The solar plexus absorbs each energy that is sent and consciously feeds the centers. Thus, comprehension of the fiery centers is the most essential task. Medical science will be able to diagnose a disease only when it knows its correspondence with cosmic energies.

239. Only through a spiritual approach can one come closer to Hierarchy. Consonance of the heart and understanding of the power of Service must underlie the foundation of all beginnings. Each deviation from the focus will become a target for a hostile arrow. Therefore one can become a co-worker only by defending the great Focus. Verily, only thus can one attain!

240. When people shall investigate not only fires and rays but also human secretions, then one may think of a change of the body. It is strange that people understand the powerful chemical processes that take place in their organisms and at the same time consider the products of these processes only as refuse. One can see how powerful is the blood or saliva. One can see what unusual strength the blood of the vegetable kingdom, valerian, transmits to a plant. Equally powerful

are saliva and the other secretions of the glands. But one must observe the causes of increase and decrease of the reaction of the energy of these products. The saliva of wrath is poisonous, and the saliva of benevolence is beneficial. Is it not important to investigate such generally known manifestations, for which mechanical equipment cannot be substituted? Thus we shall again approach the lost knowledge regarding the substance of psychic energy, that mysterious Atma, which in ancient medical science was found in using the products of the glands. One must be able to oppose the fiery element by Atma, which is incombustible.

241. Atma must be understood as the energy of space purified by unceasing rotation, like a great churning. One must understand how the spirit and Atma cooperate like electron and proton. It is not Our custom to deliver a course on chemistry and biochemistry, but Our task is to provide the impetus and to direct attention to the greatest need and danger. Just now is perhaps the most dangerous time! One can withstand it not only by the strength of the spirit but also by means of one's organism.

242. Certainly the dark force fears most of all the affirmation of Light. All servitors of darkness intensify their forces when the servitor of Light imbues space with the Decree of the Lords. Humanity knows great examples of such battle and victory of Light. Certainly each one receives a Teacher in accordance with his own consciousness. It is the same with the chain of the dark ones, who are filled with the consciousness of evil, setting up their decision against Light. Thus, the forces are strained in Cosmos by diverse affirmations. Therefore one may affirm that Light conquers darkness. Thus the life of Infinity is built.

243. The legend about St. Christopher corresponds

to the legend about the Burden of the World. People must feel a certain burden near those boundaries where the spirit realizes the manifestation of Infinity. The other kingdoms of nature do not know this anguish, because they have not reached the stage of a perceptive consciousness. Indeed, the consciousnesses of many people are also asleep. But the Burden of the World is unavoidable for those who have already pondered about the far-off worlds.

244. The same people will understand that silence is not inaction. When I advise silence, it does not mean to merge into sleep, but on the contrary, to resound to the Might of Hierarchy. One must train all seven-year-olds to remember the Hierarchy, because after the seventh year the consciousness already acquires traces indelible for the entire lifetime.

245. There are many shiftings in space, and it is not astonishing that the currents are transmitted by new rhythms. These rhythms are quite difficult because they arise from incidental vibrations during collisions with the currents of space; the wave is ten strokes too long and on account of this is fatiguing. Moreover, it is impossible to foresee the generation of new nebulae, because they are created by the shifting of the currents. One can perceive the newly formed nebulae only at the kindling of the last fires.

246. In cosmic creativeness the Spatial Fire approaches the earthly firmament when all corresponding energies are tensed. Creativeness can enter life only when all levers are impelled toward shifting. Therefore each shifting of a nation is manifested conformingly, and the old is replaced by a new course. Therefore the karma of each shifting is ordained by an entire sequence of corresponding affirmations. The earthly crust carries many traces of karma, and they must be shifted for renovation. Therefore humanity must strive conformably for renovation. The greatest and true path is Hierarchy.

247. Thus, during cosmic shiftings a new keynote must definitely resound. Each step has its own manifested karma. For the new Manvantara one must saturate space with the call to Hierarchy. Only thus can the best foundations of Existence enter into life. Hence, Our Teaching is so vital; hence, Our Hierarchy is so mighty; hence, the great Focus is given, for everything is grouped around the seed, and each step has its own saturation.

248. Each ploughman will say that he wants the plough that makes the largest and deepest furrow. Indeed, why cross the field twice, and why not reach the fertile strata? Let the depth of the furrow be reverence to Hierarchy and the width of the furrow be steadfastness of motion. Let us watch where there is a lack of reverence for Hierarchy and where non-fulfillment of Commands. Let us notice where there is readiness to retreat. Each harm must be eradicated. Rising in spirit one should watch where are the unprotected spots.

249. Certainly, the evolution of the spirit requires refinement, without which it is impossible to build. Each one who considers himself a server of culture must accept the affirmation of the revealed synthesis, for how are the steps of culture to be built without a cautious attitude? Therefore, each foundation must be guarded for affirmation to the world. Culture is built, not with an attitude of coarseness toward the subtle energies and thought, but by a creative attitude of caution and responsibility. Hence, while constructing, one should remember about refinement and about striving to the higher spheres. Thus the evolution of the spirit is achieved.

250. Forgetfulness, distraction, duplicity, curiosity, belong to the imperfections which must be eradicated. Any of these qualities may be regarded as treason, for out of them issues the lowest. One should understand how unavoidable for oneself are their consequences. A small consciousness is engulfed in mistakes and, trying to justify itself—in other words to lie to itself, actually sinks to the bottom. It can be observed through many lives how the garden of effects blossoms. Sooner or later one must be convinced of the harm of mistakes. The main touchstone will be the question, "Is there no treason?" One must in the end realize how manifold is treason. Besides the classical kiss, there may be found many subtle aspects of treason.

251. Each stage of development requires its own tension. So many manifestations affirmed through development are lost because of non-conformity. Therefore, for the assimilation of great plans great measures should be applied. How can one instill in a small consciousness the concept of Hierarchy! Each dwarf considers his labor the most important, but in the Service of Giants the measures must be affirmed by the spirit. Verily, one must co-measure between mighty measures and the kingdom of dwarfs. Hence, on the path it is inadmissible to apply measures corresponding to the kingdom of dwarfs. Great ways require great understanding.

252. Therefore, when striving saturates the spirit, the understanding of the need for higher measures is established correspondingly. Thus, to advance one should understand with what care Hierarchy must be regarded. Therefore, one must affirm one's consciousness upon the great concept of Hierarchy. Thus, with-

out the manifested focus there can be no attainment or construction. Creativeness can be developed only by affirmation of the focus. Thus I ordain.

253. Many legends express the danger of having several Gurus. Let us cite one of them. "One pious woman had three sons. Each of them had chosen a venerable Rishi as his Guru. But one of them conceived the idea of increasing his powers by asking two more Rishis to be his guides, though his mother had warned him of the danger of such a thoughtless action. The time came when the Rishis began to teach the three youths to fly. The third youth asked the two other Rishis to strengthen his flights, so that he might be ahead of his brothers. But the whirlwinds sent from three places crossed and the light-minded fellow was torn to pieces in the air; whereas his brothers flew safely in the direction of the Rishi chosen by them." Thus people remember the law of Hierarchy. One might adopt this law. From every standpoint of knowledge science confirms other laws of life; however, one should not look with an oblique eye.

254. Each shattering of the foundations spoils the entire web. Striving loyalty is needed like oil for levers. For Us it makes no difference why, despite loyalty, something is not done, but We often see how an already ripe chemical reaction is dissolved. Thus, one should sharpen the blade of the glaive, because success is not farther away than the length of a spear. Guard the concept of Hierarchy.

255. Construction is in need of firm foundations, and only the unwaveringness of the spirit can affirm the needed direction. Therefore, when the builders of life strain their forces for constructivity, it is always with cosmic assertion. Thus the builders of life carry the Higher Will, and the might of the fire directs the

spirit toward the Cosmic Magnet. Thus, the builders of life verily know the Higher Will. Creativeness is transmitted through the affirmation of Hierarchy, and only when the spirit can strive toward realization of the main foundations can creative correspondence be established. Verily, Hierarchy affords a creative chain and constructivity in life. That is why We so often repeat about Hierarchy. That is why We direct thoughts to the foundations of Hierarchy. That is why We intensify all forces for a full adoption of the focus. Verily, only thus can one conquer and attain the predestined.

256. It is said, "Where thy foot treads, lilies will blossom. Where thy head rests, all the sapphires of the world will gather." Thus is the benevolent Messenger spoken of. When We send a Messenger, We do not lose time in repeating the entire Teaching. But the Command will be contained in a few words, because the chosen Messenger knows the Teaching and reverences Hierarchy. To such a Messenger the sapphires and the lilies belong. One should not reiterate at the last moment, for the steed beats with its hoof, not knowing the length of the journey.

257. Certainly, the secretions serve for the most sacred acts, and not only the substance itself but its emanations participate in the creativeness of the world. What you remembered about Paracelsus and his homunculi is very characteristic, because this microcosm can be easily magnified to Macrocosm. And the Teaching about the great spiritual secretions has a great foundation. Certainly one can imagine how greatly interested We are in those organisms that have already transcended the degree of the "Lion of the Desert."

258. In cosmic constructiveness all shiftings are tensed, and each nation predetermines its Karma and

its place in evolution. According to each instance one can judge what step in our evolution was occupied by the departed nation and what step will be occupied by the nation that is being shifted. Thus the historical steps of our time are discerned, and one can trace how differently the tensions of the shiftings of peoples proceed. What holds back a nation in its historical progress? How can a nation preserve its drive to ascend? Only through Hierarchy and an understanding of the Highest Will. These levers can propel humanity to the predestined affirmation. With this consciousness one can approach cooperation with higher spheres. Only thus can the national shifting be evidenced as an ascent.

259. Thus, each spirit brings to a nation its accumulations and actions. Thus, each spirit strains its conscious impulses. The Karma of a nation can come closer to ascent when each spirit understands its responsibility. Thus, one may affirm that personal, group, and national Karma depend upon the full realization of Hierarchy. The creativeness of Our Carriers of Fires, who are sent by Us, is affirmed by Us for the betterment of life.

260. How often must the gardener water the garden entrusted to him? Certainly every day, except during a beneficent shower. When people close their shutters, the gardener weaves baskets for the ripening fruit. Verily, the shower frees the gardener from the labor of carrying water. Is it not the same with the Teaching? Certainly the foundations of the Teaching should be reiterated each day. Every hour, the Teaching should be protected from the leprosy of habit. But in the time of the whirlwind the Teaching is not in need of protection, because in it alone will the sole hope of men be found. Then they will turn their heads from Earth and perhaps for the first time perceive the far-off worlds and the heavenly Fire. The gardener calls the shower a blessing. Shall we not say the same of the whirlwind, which will force us to think of the Fire of Space and of future existence?

261. Let us not understand the cosmic whirl as do the animals, who sense something incomprehensible and try to hide in the darkness of their burrows. An enlightened consciousness does not conceal the battle from itself, and, being prepared by the Teaching, is able to break any hostile arrow against the shield of illumination. Even the crashing of the destroyed hostile blow is heard. We pity the one who receives a rebounding blow, which, according to the law, increases tenfold. Is it not wondrous to feel in life the application of the great laws of justice? One may speak of them at length, but their application in life is convincing.

262. Our constructiveness can proceed in any circumstances of life. Many times already you could have been convinced of the distressful condition of the planet. We repeat untiringly about the urgent renovation of life, but humanity is deaf. Cosmogony is served to people at their meals with soup or dessert, but not as a foundation of life. The hypotheses of many experimenters could be adopted, but the Hierarchy will not be realized. Many blows are being prepared; one must adhere to the Hierarchy with all strength! One must strain one's utter attentiveness to Our Counsels. I do not speak abstractly, but for application.

263. Each of Our Counsels was already given many times, but people's lives do not change. Yet space must be saturated, for there are many listeners. What does it matter in what body they are! All of you feel the great tension; each in his own way feels the predestined year. Therefore I say, Guard your health, preserve your

courage, because without Us there is no advance. Harken with three ears.

264. It is pointed out that spilled blood especially attracts spatial entities. This is truly so. Still we must not forget that all secretions possess the same properties. In like manner each spatial entity of equal degree is attracted to blood and saliva. Thus even an irritated skin is accessible to these entities. The lymphatism of mediums has the same property. Thus in ancient times, the priests greatly avoided lymphatic servants and disciples. For the insulation of secretions, films out of A. have been used.

The given emulsion has the same insulative quality, and it not only protects, but increases the circulation of the psychic energy. One may observe how harmlessly the emulsion alkalizes the skin, protecting it from accumulations. Thus, the emulsion externally and a powder internally will be the best armor. The lymph acquires a form of covering and even becomes beneficial. Thus, by simple means one can considerably protect oneself from undesirable surroundings.

265. For the realization of Hierarchy the broadening of understanding is necessary. Without broadening there will be neither depth nor length. Only thus will Hierarchy enter the consciousness and be applied to life. Only thus will Hierarchy transform the concept of conventionality. The battle will be transformed into an increase of energy. Slander will become a megaphone. Fatigue will indicate the need of a change of labor. Love will become a torch of Light. A gift will become an increase of power. Tenacity will mean the shortening of the path. Thus each property and quality will be transformed.

266. The manifestation of Hierarchy guarantees the transformation of the usual into the valuable and of the small into the significant. It can easily be seen how the followers of the Hierarchy were enriched with true values. Thus, some day it will be possible to publish the biographies of the votaries of the Hierarchy. A convincing picture will be revealed; but for results a whole-hearted acceptance of the Hierarchy, without reserve, is actually needed.

267. When the chalice of world events is being filled, then the fiery Chalice of an Agni Yogi is aflame. The law of correspondences acts powerfully. In these consonances the unity of the worlds is contained. Therefore, when the fiery law shifts the old affirmations, the sensitive centers resound with the world's reverberations. Thus, the unity is intensified with the reverberation of the centers.

Therefore, the Mother of Agni Yoga feels intensely the brimming of the World Chalice. Hence, the fiery Treasure must be so greatly protected. When the time of the great fulfillment is close, then the world is in tremor; when the great shifting takes place, the subtle centers reverberate. Thus, the world will remember the great consonance, and Our annals will leave to the world the fiery signs. Thus the Covenants will be fulfilled. Yes, yes, yes!

268. People hear about the application of the inner fires for future evolution and overlook the significance of the fires for the present time. It will be asked, "What is the most striking significance of the fire concealed in us?" It is difficult to conceive, but it is certain that our fire is the chief regulator of earthquakes. The kindled centers, the conductors of the Fire of Space, quench the subterranean fire. One can trace how the Great Teachers sent their apostles to the places threatened by a disturbance of the fiery balance. In the future, many experiments could be carried out in this

direction. Besides, the magnet of fire reacts also upon the human consciousness; in other words, fire has the greatest application. Fire is the most powerful conductor. Certainly the kindling of the fire is not easy, especially when the currents are so tense; but one may be sure that it is just this fire that is the talisman of the alchemists, so carefully concealed by them.

269. Contact with the Fire of Space strains all centers. Like a magnetic wave, the Fire attracts the inner fires. The current of space runs through all sensitive centers and nerves; therefore each cosmic wave is so powerfully reflected in the flaming centers. When the subterranean fire seeks an outlet, the waves of the Spatial Fire are intensified correspondingly. Few are those who can affirm themselves in the understanding of the great correspondences in Cosmos. Thus, the revealed law unites all cosmic manifestations. We must accept that might which leads us to the highest laws—the Might of Hierarchy. Yes, yes, yes!

270. Simply and powerfully, life is imbued with the great law of Hierarchy. One need only accept the entire affirmed Might, then it will be possible to establish the entire scope. Thus, consciousness should strive to the great law of Hierarchy.

271. By filling our lungs with air and establishing the rhythm of breathing, we can sustain our bodies upon the surface of the water. It is not difficult to conceive that with one more component we can walk upon water. The fires of the lungs will add the required condition. It is similar to the experiments with fire in empty globes; as they fill with gases, so the inner fire acts. One may also conceive of levitation through the fires of the lungs. The Spatial Fire blends with the kindled centers, and, like a magnet, attracts the fiery body. The Teacher points out these possibilities as conditions for the densified astral body. Verily, the Teacher mentions the fiery people at the time of experiments for the formation of a new body.

272. True, in irritation lies the chief harm to the fires. At the symptoms of irritation one is advised to inhale deeply ten times. The inhaling of prana has not only a psychic significance but also a chemical one, for prana is beneficial to the fires and also extinguishes irritation.

273. Humanity comments in its own way on each ordained affirmation. It distorts in its own way each Ordainment from Above. It applies each great principle to life in its own way. It asserts each manifested will in its own way. How can the great be contained in the small, and the cosmic in the personal? How can the great Servitor of Reason and of entire humanity be understood by a consciousness that recognizes only its own hearth? How can a self-denying Leader become affirmed in the understanding of a small daily routine? Only when a spark of devotion to Hierarchy burns in the heart will one find the Gates open. Only gratitude to the Teacher can reveal the entrance to the Gates. Each one who has chosen his own path must realize the loneliness of his orbit, because only love and devotion for Hierarchy include the spirit in the Chain of Light. Thus, each one determines his own karma. Only through Light do we approach Light.

274. People are preoccupied with the definition of the boundary between good and evil. Many legends are dedicated to this definition. It is related that in order to define this boundary an Archangel placed his resplendent glaive between good and evil. Certainly, it is harmful to remain in the region of evil, but it is likewise painful to crowd too close to the fiery blade. Yet people strive to wound themselves on this glaive.

Therefore, let us mark the people who perceive with the eye and understand with the conscious vision of the heart. They will strive far and, as it were, draw themselves to a far-off beacon. These anchors for far-off navigation are so valuable. In the tidal waves the fetid spots of evil are washed away. Especially nowadays should one cast these distant anchors. It can be seen that small distances lose their meaning. The great Plan of Unity comprises the expansion of material and spiritual dimensions.

275. Contact with the spatial current manifests a powerful resonance of the fiery centers. The contact with the Spatial Fire calls forth new tensions. Thus the greatness of consonance can be affirmed in Cosmos. How is it possible for humanity not to ponder over the great principles that guide life? To eliminate the Guiding Forces means to sever the silver thread and to exclude oneself from the Chain of Hierarchy. The planet is sick because it has lost the highest principles. Thus, one must manifest the most vital understanding of the great principles and of the silver thread which binds all worlds. Thus We affirm the principles of Hierarchy.

276. How many unnecessary manifestations people create for themselves! How many superfluous karmic impediments they create for themselves! And all this only because of unwillingness to admit the Hierarchy to their hearts. Thus, all affirmations can enter into life only when the consciousness can accept the Hierarchy. Each evil in the world is generated because of resistance to the great principle of Hierarchy. Each victory is gained only by the principle of Hierarchy. Therefore, one must be so strongly based upon the affirmed Hierarchy.

277. In reality, the inner fires are basically anal-

ogous to electric light. The greater the tension, the more intense the light. The purple star is the sign of utmost tension. You have felt the reaction of such a tension; it corresponds to Our constant tension. Take the manifestation of electricity as conforming to the Infinite. Often the profane think that the tension of the higher worlds is less than their own. "As in heaven, so on earth," and the great tension of the higher spheres is not to be compared with the earthly battle. One can easily conceive how problems are magnified in space.

278. It can be understood how much more complex are group, state, and national karmas. Their intermingling is not lessened but increased by the conventional boundaries of humanity. One can feel how aggravated is the interrelation between the powers of Light and darkness, which increases the non-conformity of the reaction of nature. You can see how greatly perturbed are the weak spirits, how greatly obsessions increase, and to what an extent these obsessions complicate karma. So, also, the earthly battle should not upset anyone, because one can understand how it is magnified in Infinity.

Is it easy, where the Chaos of the Unmanifest rages? Along the Chain of Hierarchy the strained heart can feel the reverberation of the tension of the cosmic battle.

279. During the construction of great steps one can observe how the central power gathers around itself all that is needed for evolution. Like a focal magnet, the leader of progress attracts everything to himself, sweeping away the old accumulations and creating new currents. Thus, throughout history, countries have been built by such leaders. It can be stated that by evidencing full adherence to Hierarchy any cosmic task can be fulfilled. Humanity has suffered most through its severance from the Higher Will. Only through affirmation of the great unification with the Higher Power can the fulfillment of Higher Laws be achieved. It is impossible for the acceptance of the powerful Hierarchy to be established without an understanding of the Higher Will.

Thus, each step is built by the realization of the affirmed Will, upon which all higher correspondences are intensified. Thus, so many evident possibilities can be attracted from the Treasury. The non-acceptance of the Higher Will complicates all structures. This should be remembered! Each structure is held by its focus. Hence, one must act by striving consciously toward Hierarchy.

280. Let us turn back to the concept of love. In each book a considerable place must be allotted to that fundamental concept, especially because under the concept of love much of the opposite is understood. It is correctly pointed out that love is a guiding and creative principle. This means that love must be conscious, striving, and self-denying. Creativeness requires these conditions. And if love is marked by self-enfeeblement, disintegration, and service to self, it will not be the highest concept of humanity, which extols the concept of achievement. The heart filled to the brim with love will be active, valiant, and will expand to its capacity. Such a heart can pray without words and can bathe in bliss. How greatly in need is humanity of the realization of the fire of love! A purple star of the highest tension will correspond to this fire.

281. It is necessary to realize very exactly the fundamental concepts of Be-ness. The love of achievement is not austere for those aflame in heart, but it frightens those who love their weaknesses and who waver while embracing their own illusionary "I." Love that can move worlds does not resemble the love upon the marshes, where the bones of outworn remains are decaying. Above the marshes are the will-o'-the-wisps of decay, but the eternal creative fire of the heart does not wander, it impetuously ascends by the steps of Hierarchy to the Highest Light. Love is the leading creative principle.

Unbearable is the Almighty Light, but Hierarchy is the link to that dazzling Summit. The Hierarchy leads an illumined spirit to that point where one might even be blinded. Love is the crown of Light.

282. The foundation upon which everything is built must be protected from disintegration. The foundation that upholds everything must be enhanced by all the best strivings; for upon the stones of the foundation stands the structure; for upon the foundation stands each affirmation. How, then, shall people treat the foundations, without realizing that the main thing is the cornerstone? So much has been destroyed by man, because of his failure to appreciate his treasures, and by his exposing the most essential to the hail storm! Thus, humanity must understand the great significance of the power of the foundation and must accept Hierarchy with its whole spirit.

283. During the hour of human injustice, recall spatial justice. Verily, there exist maps of the highest mountains, but none of the deepest abysses. Even those who are far from flights of the spirit prefer summits to abysses. If a caravan is maintained according to the weakest member, history is based upon the most powerful ones. Thus, let us remember about this wondrous substance which selects that which is most precious for evolution. If we are certain that we serve evolution, we can rely upon the justice of space. Yet the same justice prescribes necessary caution toward the black forces.

Usually they do not approach directly; they choose not less than three intercessors. They know that their auras can be easily detected, and therefore they choose a consecutive chain of succession, establishing the gradation very subtly. Not casually do We speak of the varieties of treason.

284. When I speak of the black ones I advise paying attention to their subtle methods, and discerning how patiently they creep to the goal and how they choose shoulders behind which to screen themselves. You do not see the black ones, but the grey ones and almost white ones. However, this telegraph requires great attention.

285. Cancer can be treated by psychic energy, since lack of psychic energy in the blood generates the disease. Often psychic energy is exhausted as a result of spiritual outpouring, as was the case with Ramakrishna and other spiritual Teachers. Certainly, they possessed an enormous amount of it, but, despatching it to far-off distances, they could remain for a while without its protection. Precisely closeness to Hierarchy is needed in such cases, because even great Spiritual Toilers, in their self-abnegation sometimes expend their forces beyond a legitimate extent. Thus, for evolution We reiterate about Hierarchy, in order to affirm a goal-fitting application of one's forces to the Chain of the Highest Ones. Therefore, I say, Guard your health, in order to adhere to the Hierarchy even by this means.

286. The Higher Will—who remembers it? Who will ponder upon what is affirmed by the Higher Will? Many reiterate that the manifestation of the wishes of the Higher Will is comprehensible to them. But humanity perceives only its own direction, not considering the course of evolution. Hence there are so many accumulations of opposite courses. And humanity has lost its defense, because it proceeds contrary to the Higher Will. Thus, the entire cosmic significance of the Higher Will should be understood.

287. Let us turn to devotion. This concept is also subject to many distortions. Devotion does not resemble a windmill, or a hired singer of praises. Rather, it resembles a firm tower upon a summit, which the enemies avoid in awe, but in whose chambers a shelter is ever prepared for a friend. Devotion is the opposite of doubt, which is nothing but ignorance. It means that devotion rests upon enlightenment. Thus, validity of learning is akin to devotion. It is not credulity, not levity, but firmness and steadfastness. Truly, the tower of devotion is not constructed by haphazard toil or by petty decisiveness; and devotion can be violated only by perfidy, which is the same as betrayal. But valuable are the towers of devotion! Such ashrams, like magnets, attract powerful hearts; they are nurseries of spirituality. Even material nature is transformed in the proximity of these towers.

288. The cosmic laws are little understood by humanity. In life all organizations clash with Cosmos. Thus, humanity accepts only a few of the visible effects, but refuses to accept the treasures of Cosmos. The causes of this are lack of faith and ignorance. Therefore disunion has taken place. How can one affirm the cosmic laws when such a wall of denial has risen before humanity? Thus, each great law corresponds to life and to the leading laws. Thus, one can build upon the Chain of Hierarchy, which leads to the summit of manifest Beauty.

289. The principles of the affirmation of cosmic laws are enrooted in the spirit. Striving toward Service always opens the revealed Gates. Thus, Our victory is always brought into life by the law of striving and invincibility of the spirit. Thus the predestined will be fulfilled. So I affirm! Thus, when the focus affirmed by Us shall be verily guarded, the Magnet will act.

290. A physician usually says to his patient, "When summer comes you will go to the country, into the sun. You will be regenerated by the mountain wind or the sea breeze." Even an earthly physician cures by projecting into the future. Karma is the sickness of the past. Its cure lies in the future. Precisely, he who wishes to be liberated from the past should strive into the future. Striving with one's entire being protects one from downfalls; take for example the moving heavenly bodies. Thus, remember that I have pointed out how to walk upon the water, but I have never said that one can stand upon it. Karma can be changed by an irresistible striving.

291. Motion into the future is similar to the movement of a flame. It is amazing how the fire, at times visibly and at times invisibly, lives, while vibrating and preserving the balance of the world. Thus let us strive into the future, because sustained by the fiery element we shall not fail. But the fire can be invoked only by an action of the spirit. Thus, let us apply the higher laws to the earthly plan. One may even change karma, which means that one can change all earthly conditions by striving into the future. Apply My Command to life. The particles of precious energies adhere only to him who strives.

292. The building of the great steps of evolution takes place through unusual ways. Each new step always brings to humanity an affirmation which impels thought to new and mighty possibilities. Thus, the Highest Will also intensifies each energy in accordance with the Cosmic Magnet. There is no affirmation that would not be fulfilled if sent by the Highest Will.

There is no striving that would not be acknowledged if sent by the Highest Will. Therefore, humanity must strive only to Hierarchy. Verily, in this cosmic concept are contained all possibilities of constructiveness.

293. Humanity grows weak to such an extent, because it evidences disunion with the Highest Will. Therefore We so powerfully affirm the focus, for without the center the Highest Will cannot be accepted. Therefore We summon so powerfully to Hierarchy. Verily, we must sacredly guard the treasures. They underlie the foundations of Our Work. Each sacred creativeness is a contribution to evolution. Let us ponder upon the significance of a great thought; let us ponder upon the great might of the fires of the Tara; let us ponder upon the devotion of the heart; let us ponder upon the invincibility of those who walk in the name of the Lord.

294. Sometimes one can demonstrate the most complex laws by means of the simplest apparatus. The law of karma is complex, but take the Ruhmkorff coil or any other electric coil and you will get a graphic image of karma. The current runs along the spiral uninterruptedly, but the protective winding is subject to all external reactions; moreover each thread contacts the thread of the preceding round, carrying upon it the consequences of the past. Thus, each hour changes karma, for each hour evokes the corresponding past. Thus, one can contact the entire line of past experiences.

The same graphic example shows how the seed of the spirit is unharmed; and striving to the heights it sustains its shell without fearing the past. Verily, karma is frightening only to those who are plunged into inaction. But a striving thought is liberated from the burden of the past, and like a heavenly body is impelled forward without retracing its path. Thus, even with a difficult karma, one can achieve a useful liberation.

295. Let us see how people understand Service to the Lord and Hierarchy. He who thinks of ascending only by prayer is far from Service. He who in his labor hopes to bring the best efforts for the good of humanity must adopt the Lord with his heart. He who does not relinquish his own comfort does not know how to serve Hierarchy. He who does not accept the Indications of the Hierarchy does not understand Service. Only when the heart is ready to accept consciously the affirmation sent by the Highest Will can it be said that the realization of Service is adopted. Thus, We are no lovers of funeral rites and of empty invocations to the Lord. Thus, We venerate the striving of disciples to the Service of Hierarchy. Hence it is so easy to observe how the one who does not accept the Service in spirit venerates the Lord and Hierarchy only so long as the way is convenient to him.

Thus, We take into account each effort to remove the burden from the Hierarchy; as in the great, so in the small. Thus, in Our creativeness, We affirm reverence not in words but by deeds. Thus, We deplore it when We see reverence in words but not in action.

296. Thus, humanity is an accumulator and transmuter of the high energy which We have agreed to call psychic energy. The significance of humanity consists in its transmutation of this energy through consciousness and propelling it by way of Hierarchy into the higher spheres. The loss of the understanding of one's own predestination has thrown people back from the understanding of responsibility. Therefore, We remind again of the foundation of Existence. One must prepare oneself for the next evolution. Once again, one must draw closer to the great current and realize the principles of the renewal of life. You notice how greatly opposed We are to spiritism, but We often speak about the subtle bodies. We smile at contemporary hypnotism, but speak about rays and magnets. We advise re-examination of your pharmacopoeia, but offer a few fundamental medicines.

297. Where, then, is attention directed? It must be understood that the process toward perfection lies at the basis of evolution. It summons one to simplification and to direct communion with higher worlds. It can be seen how pranayama and other artificial methods of various yogas can be replaced by a simple, fiery heart. Certainly this simplicity is relative. The flaming fiery path leads to it. Yet it brings into life precisely that which was rejected as abstraction and fiction. I consider that each striving to knowledge should be speedily brought to fulfillment. People ask why We do not compel the striving toward evolution. But even a plain nurse tells a child, "Be like a grown-up, find by yourself!"

298. When humanity shall realize that space is saturated by the effects of human deeds, it will be possible to cure the planet. Like gases they poison Earth and densify the atmosphere. Therefore one should ponder upon affirmation of the obvious results. Humanity has forgotten that redemption must proceed by the karmic way. Therefore each accumulated step can be transmuted by striving toward the highest law of Hierarchy. The great Chain of Hierarchy gives life to the entire world, and the acceptance of this law can open a new access to energies. Thus one can build a better step.

299. Each concept has its balance. Reverence of Hierarchy has its balance in the understanding of the pledge. If reverence of Hierarchy is directed upward, then the pledge is downward. There even exists a teraph of the pledge. You saw a pledge through a teraph. Thus, the pledge is indestructible when Hierarchy is realized. I testify that as the Teacher is immutable, so is the pledge firm. Therefore, do not pronounce the word Teacher in vain. But having pronounced it do not think of severing this silver thread. A superficial person can realize the consequences by a simple example: let him firmly attach to the wall a twisted rubber band, and let him, with closed eyes, pull it with all his strength—a bruise, not at all supernatural, will be the consequence. What then, may result from the severing of the silver thread? Once again a timorous and mischievous consciousness will speak of threats, but any law, any machine, may be the cause of unpleasantness if improperly handled.

300. Precisely with love should one teach how to deal wisely with the sacred concept of the Teacher. There are no thirty shekels for which one may hire various teachers. As wisely must one select disciples. The same silver thread binds each Teacher with each disciple. Once the pledge is pronounced it becomes the foundation of karma. Through the events of life one can observe how immutable is that which has been said. No one can give ignorance of the laws as excuse. Therefore, it is better to repeat this upon each page than to permit a heinous error, which drags behind it a loathsome wake of consequences. Not severely but vitally should the law be understood. This advice must be accepted, not in words, but by the heart. Not without cause do the teeth lock the tongue.

301. Majestic is the time! Remember that while Moses on the mountain was preparing the Tablets, the people below were steeped in madness; yet the calf of iniquity was destroyed when faced with the Highest Covenant.

302. People's striving is always measured by their service either to Light or darkness. By this may be judged their destination in life. Thus, the worst of all is halfway thinking and halfway striving. The destroyers always build solely upon halfway striving. There is nothing worse than a halfway servitor, for he screens himself by halfwayness. Therefore a direct enemy of Light is preferred by Us. We do not admit into the great battles the small worms that crawl in the mist. Thus, halfwayness must be avoided. One should always and in all ways avoid any intercourse with halfway people. Halfwayness shown by the disciples throws them back a millennium, and therefore one should know when to affirm one's own consciousness. Thus, the servitor of Light will not admit halfwayness.

303. It is most pernicious when halfwayness insinuates itself into one who is affirming himself upon the path, because then there results duality of thought and action. Hence, halfwayness is the enemy of the Teaching, and when We see halfwayness in relation to Hierarchy, this destructive attitude must be eradicated; for without integrity there can be no construction. Hence, the disciples must understand how important it is to have complete striving. For this one should renounce personal comfort, conceit, self-pity, self-deception, and should always remember that Hierarchy must not be burdened. This should be remembered by those who misunderstand Service as reliance upon the Lord and the Hierarchy.

304. The word Mahatma is translated as Great Soul. Some imagine the Mahatmas as a completely distinct race. One should not conceive a Great Soul to be entirely distinct. Each Mahatma began his ascent from the very midst of the people, having only dared to choose the difficult path of the Great Soul. And, besides daring, he found in his heart indignation of spirit, for how else can the fires be kindled? Upon these fires the precious substance of the secretions is transmuted into a healing substance. One can see how the saliva of a fiery being can remove an inflammation and restore the vital energy to numb centers. Alongside the sacred property of secretions stands the healing power of the laying on of hands. It is instructive to compare the secretions of men having dormant centers with the ejection of the fiery substance. If I advise medicines made from plants for common organisms, then for the more knowing ones there is a powerful laboratory of sacred fiery secretions.

305. My latest book will be understood by few. Who will comprehend the sacred quality of the saliva of the Savior or the laying on of the hands of Moses? People are not accustomed to appreciate a fiery heart. The book can help those who have already sensed the rise of the solar serpent. It winds its coils amidst the fiery ejections. It is impossible to imagine the affirmation of the subterranean fires without the eruption of the fires of the heart. You know about the usual ejections of the Yogi, which cannot be replaced by anything else, for this gas of the fire must be released and must blend with the Fire of Space. But the Yogis seldom attain this manifestation of confluence with the Cosmic Fire. We call this stage a holy one, for the light of the fire of the higher worlds is blended with the rays of planetary Yogis. This is the shortest path to the Mahatmas.

Do not fear tension, this is the same path. Do not be disturbed by anguish, it comes from fire. Do not be angry, for the heart dislikes this root.

306. When events pile up, the subterranean fire is impelled accordingly. Thus, when the shifting of forces takes place, one should pay attention to the cosmic fires. In one case there is regeneration, in the other, shifting. Everywhere the cosmic manifestations take place, and the Spatial Fire imbues each transitory process. People's power is nurtured by a corresponding spirit, and the same power of attraction unites the shiftings of nations. Therefore, it can be said that the tension of Cosmos is transmitted to all countries. Thus, humanity cannot sever itself from the general affirmation. Hence, the highest law impels to the General Good; and the human spirit is in need of striving to the higher law.

307. Therefore, humanity must understand the beauty of the higher laws. What, then, will indicate the path to creativeness, if not true understanding and veneration of the Hierarchy? What, then, will attract the spirit to the Highest, if not adherence to the law of Hierarchy? What, then, will direct the spirit toward the manifestation of Truth, if not understanding of Hierarchy? Therefore, for a higher understanding one must accept Hierarchy with one's heart and strive irresistibly to the highest law of Hierarchy.

308. An experienced sailor frowns at a dead calm of the sea, foreseeing the gathering of a storm, and smiles at the blustering wind, perceiving a successful navigation. Of such a sailor it is said that he knows the sea. We say that he knows life if he knows how to understand the difference between the inner and outer manifestations. Some fools shout, "Rebellion!" when they hear the cry of a pottery vender, and exult at the quiet when they see a closed market. Our way is to teach and to observe how different is the thought of dissolute people. Classes for thinking and the observation of life processes should be established in schools. It may often be noticed that a child understands the hidden meaning of an occurrence better than an adult.

Only according to inner feeling can we approach a just evaluation. We accept a calm surface before a storm, and we do not pay attention to the blowing curtains at the doors. Thus, the formation of events will be understood.

309. When the Forces of Light and darkness are fighting, the orbit of each camp is being established. That which nurtures the camp of Light will certainly be the center of tension, and the goal of Light will be the target for darkness. Therefore, when the Forces are in conflict, everything pertaining to the center should be guarded. The main Fire of Space will abide in the center, and the protecting net should be guarded. Thus, the orbit of Light engulfs darkness.

310. When the Forces of Light and darkness are strained, health must be guarded, because the Fire of Space is raging and darkness is tense. But in all Our manifestations one should perceive victory. When everything crumbles that is old and not applicable for evolution and for the Epoch of Fire, one anchor remains, which will save humanity—the anchor of Hierarchy, which will unite the entire chain and give the entire power. Thus, one should become limitlessly affirmed in Hierarchy.

311. Let us observe how the black ones labor. It is necessary to observe their peculiar habits. They are not indignant about a nonentity. They consider that the first steps of service are particularly useful for them. A nonentity is negligible even in treason. Treason is precisely the main basis of undermining by the black ones. For treason, one must know something. This relative knowledge, not strengthened by devotion, may be found on the first steps. One must know that condemnation acts like fire upon a wavering devotion. It is sad to observe with what unnoticeable deviations the disciple begins to steep himself in indifference, finding eloquent justifications. Like the blade of a knife, the heart loses its protective net. Without its sheath, the blade injures the carrier himself; and such spurs do not lead to achievement, they lead only to irritation. If one day has passed successfully in demeaning the Teacher, why may not tomorrow also be blazing with blasphemy against the Highest? And if the silver thread is broken, the blade of ossification is already irrevocably sharpened.

312. It is necessary to observe the wavering ones, for the contagion from them is great. Often they themselves are about to be submerged in the black agglomeration, yet the blasphemy disseminated by them wounds many innocent ones. You arm yourself rightly against indifference; it corrodes all beginnings, and what fires are possible from the frigidity of indifference? Also, the affirmations of the Teacher are like the watering of flowers. The watered garden will not wither. We are concerned with advancing. We affirm new dimensions! Indifference to Our affirmations is impermissible!

313. When the spirit is filled with striving, there is no place for indifference. When the spirit is aflame, there is no place for indifference. This quality provides immunity to indifference. Only when the spirit tends to egoism can its death occur. Therefore, one should flamingly protect the spirit from indifference where the evil generated by neglected striving will nestle, whence this evil will inflict a blow that will bear fruit. It is difficult to detect the root of evil generated by indifference. Only in endless vigilant striving can one find protection for construction. Hence, while constructing great works, one must understand that egoism and indifference are inadmissible.

Therefore, We demand that the first thought be dedicated to the Teacher. Is it possible to succeed when the disciple puts himself in the first place? Are We not building all upon a great Name? Did We not put Beauty at the foundation? We have given the great foundations for the world. Therefore each thought must be valued as the foundation of a great structure. Verily, the future is great!

314. Amidst the concepts of courage, the most invincible is the courage of the flaming heart when, with full decisiveness, with full realization of achievement, the warrior knows only the path of advance. To this achievement of courage only the extreme degree of the courage of desperation is comparable. With the same speed with which the courage of the flaming heart overcomes the future, desperation flees from the past. Thus, where the courage of the flaming heart is lacking, let there be the courage of desperation. Only thus can the warrior gain victory when the offensive is great. All other aspects of courage are of no significance, because in them will be halfwayness. This quality, next to cowardice and treason, must be avoided.

315. The reorganization of the world intensifies all the forces of Cosmos. If humanity would understand that reorganization requires the striving of the spirit, it would be easy to establish equilibrium in the world. But the nations do not ponder about what to place upon the scales and where is the balance; hence the chaos of thinking is so destructive to humanity, and thus the dislocated nations sink to the depths without taking measures for spiritual transmutation. Therefore, it is time to ponder the establishing of spiritual quests. When the cosmic perturbations require a powerful tension, humanity must know where to look for the center of salvation.

Therefore, the quest for a spiritual center will lead unavoidably to Hierarchy. Humanity has lost the necessary formula for salvation. Hence, the anchor for salvation is the focus of Hierarchy. Only a conscious quest and the affirmation of Hierarchy will afford salvation. Yes, yes, yes! Therefore, We gave the basis for actions and works that are founded on Beauty.

316. Healing through the fragrance of flowers, resins, and seeds goes back to hoary antiquity. Thus, a rose not only possesses a similarity to musk but also prevents imperil. A garden of roses was considered by the ancients as a place of inspiration. Freesias are beneficial for the sympathetic nervous system, which vibrates so much in a Yogi. The seeds of barley are unsurpassed for the lungs. You know already about mint, about the resin of cedar and other resins. Perfumes are now bereft of meaning like all other desecrated values, yet the origin of fragrance underlies a useful but forgotten knowledge. Certainly the poisons of antiquity were very subtle. The newly invented narcotics are comparatively crude; chiefly, they destroy the intellect—in other words, precisely that which sustains the balance in all psychic experiments. A flaming heart without spiritual balance is an impossibility. Thus one must remember all details that bring one close to Hierarchy.

317. The disciples on the path of Service must apply all the best strivings of their spirit and consciousness. While creating, one should understand that only the application of the best actions affords corresponding results. Thus, let us not expect beautiful results where the spirit has not applied its best strivings. Often people wonder why their undertakings are unsuccessful. Let us say then, Did you apply all your best impulses? Did not light-mindedness, the dullness of inflexibility, negligence, and lack of ardor for the Hierarchy intrude themselves? Thus, one may expect correspondence based upon cause and effect. Thus, one must understand that each irresponsible action, each non-goalfitting deed, may bring many unnecessary and harmful consequences. Thus, the disciples on the path must display their best strivings and ardor to the Hierarchy.

318. Hence one must chiefly develop one's vigilance and watch untiringly the creativeness surrounding the Sacred Hierarchy. Only when disciples shall attain this quality may one hope that the predestined success will come. Therefore, one should manifest an extreme conscientiousness and vigilance toward all that occurs around the Focus. Each unnoticed mistake will yield its own blossom.

319. It is asked why We so often delay in destroying the enemies. There are many reasons. Let us name two: the first—karmic conditions. It is easy to harm the near ones by touching an enemy bound to them by karma. This may be likened to most delicate surgery when a surgeon does not amputate a sick limb because of the danger attendant upon severing an artery. With the karmic bonds the interacting relationship is unusually complex. We consider it more useful to insulate the dangerous fellow traveler than to obstruct the entire caravan. The second reason is that enemies are the source of tension of energy. Nothing can so greatly increase the energy as counterattack. Therefore, why invent artificial obstacles when the dark ones attempt with all their strength to increase our energy?!

320. What undertakings enter into life without great tension? Each creative step is the affirmation of great battles. Each battle has its predestination, and each design its significance. Thus, those who walk along with the Powers of Light must know that without a tense battle there is no victory. Thus, when the step of great victory is being affirmed, the disciples of Light must feel entire invincibility of the spirit and entire steadfastness of actions. When the affirmation of great foundations was given to humanity, each tension was accepted as a further impulse for new structures. Thus, in evolution each banner has been affirmed by the greatness of the steadfastness manifested. Verily, only thus can one conquer!

321. One can compare the process of the inner fires with some parallels of physical fire. Let us take the flame under a blowpipe. Observe how, under pressure, the flame loses its yellow tone and through blue becomes silver and purple. Besides, let us notice how the flame inclines. Our fires are similarly strained under the pressure of the cosmic whirl. Those rare manifestations should be recorded, for they testify to participation in the cosmic battle. Few can pride themselves upon such participation. Not a chaotic tremor, but a vanguard of the hosts of Light is required for the piercing of darkness. And how blessed is the pressing whirl, which impels us into constructive battle! New thoughts may be realized in this battle, however, one should know the direction of the blow, and this We point out!

322. Hierarchy and the creation of a new consciousness are affirmed as the cornerstone of evolution. Each day one can observe the evidence of such progress. But people seldom synthesize these many-colored petals of the Fire Blossom. Courage is lacking to acknowledge oneself as living upon the ruins of the old world. Yet even a woodcutter knows in what direction the tree will fall, for he does not want to be crushed. On the contrary, he quietly calculates the amount of new

building material and fuel. Thus, one must rejoice at the cosmic battle!

323. If people would understand upon what the earthly priority is built, verily, the highest principles could be given. But who has pondered upon the principle of creative impulses? When isolation takes place, and the law asserted by the right of the great Be-ness is infringed, then, indeed, the main foundation is destroyed. Even insects know the greatness of Hierarchy. The knowledge of the foundations of life can transform life, hence only the greatness of the law of Hierarchy will give to humanity the striving to the highest steps of evolution.

324. Hence, the knowledge of the spirit is such a powerful guide, for it will always lead to the foundations of Existence. Thus, one should adopt the concept of Hierarchy as the highest Service. Thus, the knowledge of the spirit directs the disciples on the path to Hierarchy. Thus, with the entire strength of one's spirit, one should unfurl the Banner of Peace, in which are contained all the abutments of culture.

325. A poorly developed mind always stumbles at a seeming contradiction, it cannot reconcile Hierarchy with resourceful independent activity. Certainly, without synthesis the most monogenic conceptions will fall apart like brickwork without cement. The realization of synthesis will be like a step toward the transformation of the race. The remark about the immortality of unicellular organisms is correct. But with what can one bring into unity our heterogeneous elements? One can eliminate a multitude of artificial means, bringing to life the dormant crystals of psychic energy. One may think of it as our origin. Only united understanding of conscious striving toward the affirmation of ascent generates the power of transmutation. Do not think

this an abstraction; I advise accepting it as necessary for the ascent of the race.

326. Synthesis must be understood as the apparatus of the laboratory of life. Let us remember this definition. The mind that has achieved the stage of synthesis becomes productive, moral, unifying, non-irritable, capable of manifesting patient cooperation with Hierarchy. How can one explain the advantage of synthesis to one who does not ponder upon Eternity and stupidly shuts himself off from all calls? He will never understand that what is said also concerns him. Satisfied, he will garb himself in a suit approved by a tailor and be at ease, having acknowledged the tailor's hierarchy. But let us not offend the tailor because people have invented many disgusting hierarchies.

327. The vibration of objects may come from the pressure of psychic energy. The vibrations of light may also reflect upon the surroundings. Thus is so-called magnetism transmitted. Man is borne by vibrations to a like at-onement of receptivity and harmony.

328. How difficult it is for people to realize what determines their own welfare. They think that they create; they think that they labor; they think that nothing will take place without them. They think that in them lies the foundation. Woe to those who take credit for that which does not issue from themselves, for these servitors of darkness are verily the destroyers of luminous inceptions. Certainly the attempts of these dark ones only determine their own destruction, for Light is unconquerable. Thus self-destruction occurs where there is disobedience to the Hierarchy of Light. Thus, the attributing of creativeness to themselves by the dark ones has a reason, because verily the jinns have affirmed themselves as co-workers of Light. Each evil intention is the affirmation of victory.

329. Is it possible that the dark ones are blind, not wishing to show understanding of Hierarchy? Is it possible that the assertion of the Higher Law is not acknowledged as the only salvation? How important it is at such a decisive time to understand the law of Hierarchy! Thus, let traitors ponder. Thus, let the servitors of darkness, who are opposing Hierarchy, ponder. Whoever slanders Hierarchy is the greatest traitor.

330. If one combines the complete responsibility of the physician, judge, priest, teacher, architect, and lawmaker, one arrives at a part of the responsibility of a Hierarch. But just a part. For besides the earthly responsibility, He also belongs to the subtle and mental worlds. We never summon anyone to don the armor of a Hierarch, because only the spirit itself can choose such a responsibility. The seed of the Hierarch is generated according to a certain ray. Verily, the might of ascent has no fear of responsibility before the three worlds. This courage is like a link between the worlds, like the pillar of the Covenant, like the Light, all-penetrating! Thus, facing the throne of responsibility, the wings of achievement glow.

331. Without culture there can be no international agreement or mutual understanding. Without culture the people's understanding cannot embrace all needs of evolution. Therefore the Banner of Peace comprises all subtle concepts that will lead nations to the understanding of culture. Humanity does not understand how to manifest reverence for that which comprises immortality of spirit. The Banner of Peace will bring the understanding of this lofty significance. Humanity cannot flourish without the knowledge of the greatness of culture. The Banner of Peace will open the gates to a better future. When countries are on the way to destruction, then even those who are spiritually depleted must understand in what the ascent consists. Verily, salvation lies in culture. Thus, the Banner of Peace brings a better future.

332. Let people become accustomed to ejecting from their lives a multitude of petty lies and to learning to apply truth to life. Nothing is as destructive as a consciously injurious distortion of reality. It disturbs the rhythm of Cosmos. The subterranean fire dominates by the counter-current of its rhythm.

333. With the cooperation of all energies the preordained structure can be built. It is the same in human constructiveness. It should be remembered that positive forces create under the pressure of negative ones, and the creativeness of Light is saturated by the tension of the manifested pressures. Thus, creativeness in the Name of the Lords certainly calls forth tension. Hence, precisely Service to Light asserts such a tension of cosmic potencies. When such a mighty construction is being affirmed, how is it possible that the shifting forces should not be opposed?

334. Verily, the Banner of Peace will unite all cultural tasks and will give the world the achievement that is so needed. Therefore, those who carry a striving quest will respond to all affirmations. The nations will verily unite under this Banner.

335. Humanity must carry out a multitude of urgent experiments. Imperil must not only be recognized as the calamity of the departing race but the contagion of imperil should also be studied. It will be possible to ascertain that imperil acts at far distances and can affect the subtle body. Imperil clashes like a dissonance with the Fire of Space. People who depart from Earth with a store of imperil create for themselves a torturous existence; the Fire of Space rushes upon them, for harmony means adherence to the

foundations. Each opposition to the foundations calls forth the counteraction of the Fire of Space. Thus, one should admit that personal irritation is an excrescence of the departing ones. But it must be noted that people often do not wish to heed their own irritation, though the dangerous poison does not diminish because of that.

336. Thus, one should investigate impeding elements with all means. One must understand in what consists harmony with the foundations of Existence. In what lies the progress of a spirit who is gradually becoming accustomed to existing above the world and to labor without end? Also, the sacred pains should be understood as signs of the flights of the spirit into the region which binds the worlds. Thus, it is easy to understand that involution has deprived humanity of some acknowledged qualities, and one should manifest much of the primary energy, in order to weave again the torn web of Assurgina. But praise to the courageous, daring, and striving ones!

337. The time when the Fire Blossom is manifest cannot be an easy one. The Banner of Peace is not presented at the bazaar. Thus, let us be united in one unconquerable striving.

338. How does humanity expect to approach the Highest without acknowledging the entrusted earthly representatives of Hierarchy? How can a link be established if humanity does not admit the greatness of the Chain of Hierarchy? Thinking is infected so extensively by the poison of conceit that the entire cosmic balance is disturbed. Thus, on the way to Us one should adopt all the affirmations concerning Hierarchy as an anchor of salvation. Verily, Hierarchy is like a wondrous Light for humanity! As a mighty Shield, Hierarchy stands on watch! Hierarchy is affirmed as the link between the worlds!

339. Therefore the most heinous is apostasy and demeaning of the Teacher. Thus, when We introduce into life a new affirmation, one should strive with the entire spirit on the path of fulfillment of the Highest Will. Hence, when We affirm the great significance of the Banner of Peace, it must be adopted in spirit. Verily, thus the salvation of the world will come. The time is great! The time is significant!

340. Wisely is ordained the bliss of him who sacrifices his soul for his neighbor. Often this commandment is applied to the sacrifice of one's life, yet it is not said of life or body, but of the spirit. Thus a most difficult and lengthy task is given. In order to give one's soul one should cultivate, expand, and refine it, then it can be given for the salvation of one's neighbor. Thus the wisdom of the Commandment should be understood and consciously applied. It is also said, "Follow Me." Thus will speak each Hierarch, affirming a progressive motion. He cannot turn back, otherwise the leading star will be hidden behind the rock.

It is not correct to think of the humility of a Hierarch—humility ahead and the Command behind. Likewise, the concept of Hierarchy is clearly expressed in the words of the Apostle about the Comforter. This advice should be similarly understood, because inaction in sorrow is not indicated, but consolation is prepared through achievement. Thus, even the best Teachings are obscured by not acknowledging that which is imperceptible to earthly sight.

341. How is responsibility understood by the many? How little do people ponder upon the great affirmation of responsibility! The one who accepts responsibility with obvious light-mindedness or with selfish desires is subject to a terrible karma. When the great Service for the good of humanity is given, responsibility should be carried accordingly. When Our vessel is in the hands of the Carrier, it means that dignity should be preserved, in order that the wondrous vessel may keep its wings. Verily, it is befitting that responsibility be carried by a tempered spirit and with the entire solicitude of the heart.

342. Individuality and egoism are like birth and death. The building of individuality manifests the conception of a New World, whereas egoism can mirror itself in the dead volcanoes of the moon. Not only does egoism deaden itself, it strikes the surroundings with sterility, where as individuality kindles fires in all adjacent camps. Cooperation is the crown of individuality, but the scourge of egoism is like the sting of a scorpion. Can one rely upon egoism? No more than upon a viper! But true individuality contains in itself the foundation of universal justice. We must gather individualities; for a new diamond is in need of cutting, but egoism must pass through many incarnations. Indeed, this law may also be changed by the fire of the heart. Therefore, we can advise those adhering to egoism to be kindled by the proximity of a fiery heart.

343. Not without purpose do We kindle the beacons of the fiery heart as a refuge for travelers. It is not easy for the flaming heart, yet it sacrifices itself for its neighbors, which reveals the justice of the Commandment of Bliss. But joy is a special wisdom.

344. At the time of world reconstruction one can hold fast only through affirmation of the New World. The ascertainment of the manifested decision can enter life only through great understanding of world regeneration by way of the great law of Hierarchy. Therefore, those who seek the New World must strive to the confirmation of the Decree of Hierarchy, which directs through the appointed Hierarchy. Only thus can balance be established in the world. Only a flamingly guiding Heart will manifest salvation. Thus, the world is in need of the affirmation of the law of Hierarchy!

Thus Hierarchy is lawfully affirmed during the shifting of countries and the substitution of fire for all that departs. Therefore it is so urgent to adopt the law of Hierarchy, for without the chain the great ladder of ascent cannot be constructed. Thus, the affirmation of the greatness of the law of Hierarchy must be adopted fierily.

345. Do not be perturbed by the necessity for seeming repetitions. In the first place, nothing is repeated. Even the same words appear completely different at different times. Secondly, one should reiterate day and night about Hierarchy. You are right that the hierarchy of thralldom is ended, but the emergence of a realized Hierarchy is followed by human sufferings. There is too much slavery in the world, and each flame of consciousness is too oppressed. Slavery and a consciously realized Hierarchy are like day and night. Hence do not be dissuaded from repeating—a consciousness of Hierarchy, Hierarchy of freedom, Hierarchy of knowledge, Hierarchy of Light. Let those scoff who are ignorant of the inception of the New World, for each concept of a New World frightens them. Is not Infinity terrifying to them? Is not Hierarchy burdensome for them? Being ignorant despots themselves, they do not understand the constructiveness of Hierarchy. Being cowards themselves, they are horrified in the face of an achievement. Thus, let us place upon the scales the most urgent concepts of the great approaching Age—Infinity and Hierarchy.

346. When a step of evolution is being built the dark ones intensify all their cunning, because Light is unbearable to them, and, sensing their doom, the dark ones cling to the measures most stifling for them. During each new great Epoch the same pressure of forces is repeated. But a more teeming period has not been known to history, for the Epoch of Fire comprises all cosmic actions. Thus, the vigil must be fiery.

347. Many pillars of salt are spread upon the face of Earth. Not only did Lot's wife turn back to the past but numberless are those who have looked back. What did they expect to see in the burning city? Perhaps they wished to bid farewell to the old temple? Perhaps they looked for their cozy hearth? Perhaps they looked in anticipation of seeing the house of their hated neighbor collapse? Certainly, the past chained them for a long time. Thus, one must strive onward for enlightenment and health and for the strength of the future. Thus it should be always; but there may be cosmic knots when an impetuous onward motion is urgent. One should not be disconcerted and mourn over the past. Even mistakes are obvious, yet the caravan does not wait, and the very events press onward. We hurry, and We summon to hasten. The future is crowded, but there is no darkness ahead!

348. Leave all the past to Us and think only of the future. Let us not take anything useless from the past; let us not burden our consciousness by anything. I, Myself, will put away and will remember all that is valuable! Events propel one into the future. Therefore Hierarchy must be understood as a life belt; so, also, the sign of the Mother of the World may be understood. Do not be disturbed, for I will turn all to usefulness. We shall shout into the ears of the faint-hearted—Hierarchy!!! The Teaching is given at the imperative hour, and one must have the ears of an ass not to hear the thunder. It is useful to rejoice before the victory. Let us rejoice, and thus unite ourselves with the joy of the Lord.

349. Life-activity is sustained by the subtle energies of the organism. People get accustomed with difficulty to the realization of the subtle energies and to the activity of all the imperceptible forces. Hence a great disunion with Cosmos occurs, and the physical body is greatly limited by the basic properties of matter instead of developing the subtlety of receptivity. People sense so little the vibrations of cosmic forces, and they display little discrimination as to where is contained subtle cognizance! A spirit striving to the highest spheres knows that a magnetic bond exists between the subtle energies and manifests concordance with all spatial pressures. Thus, the new generation must be brought up on the understanding of the subtle energies, for the vibrations of space are nearing Earth, and the affirmation of the New Epoch will bring the shifting of many manifestations. Thus the subtle bodies will assimilate all the energies that are sent.

350. Thus, the epochs of the manifestation of Fire have always been followed by perturbations, because the spiritual consciousness was shifted, together with the cosmic changes. Hence, during the Epoch of Fire the most important thing is subtle receptivity. During the Epoch of Fire, the Hierarchy is followed by an impetuous torrent of growth of the spirit of people, and because the law of Hierarchy has not been adopted by nations, such shiftings of peoples occur. Thus, the Epoch of Fire is the Epoch of Hierarchy!

351. Hierarchy must be adopted as an evolutionary system. To those spirits who have not yet outlived slavery it should be repeated that Hierarchy differs completely from despotism. Even a chimney-sweep must climb to the roof in order to clean the flues. This cannot be done from below. One cannot compose a symphony without one key for all instruments. Many analogies may be quoted, beginning with a jest and finishing with the touching examples of bees, ants, and swans. But the best example for contemporary humanity is the comparison with impersonal chemistry. It is easy to understand that a reaction can take place only under precise conditions. Hierarchy likewise corresponds completely to the astrochemical principles, which even a neophyte of science will not deny. We justly agreed already upon the importance of the discovery of psychic energy; for the coordination of its realization Hierarchy is as indispensable as a helpful chemical process.

352. Which path is the most affirmative one on the way to Us? The most unfailing way is the path of self-sacrificing achievement. The most wondrous fire is the flame of the heart saturated with love for Hierarchy. The achievement of such a subtle heart is affirmed by Service to the Highest Hierarchy. Hence, so wondrous is the self-sacrifice of the subtle heart. The spirit-creativeness and independent action of a sensitive server fierily imbue space. Thus the subtle heart responds to all cosmic occurrences. Thus, verily, the visible reverberates with the invisible, the present with the future, and the predestined takes place. Thus the self-sacrifice of the subtle heart imbues the world with flame.

353. Verily, the sacred concept of an Arhat has been distorted. It is violated, being bereft of beauty. How dimly the understanding of the Teacher of General Good burns in the consciousness of the world! But Truth lives, and in the name of Truth We create.

Therefore, for the transformation of life one should accept Hierarchy as the beauty of Truth. Thus the subtle heart creates for cosmic evolution. Thus, one should realize the significance of the focus within the heart; thus, the great process of the subtle heart must be understood through the heart.

354. Some people cannot tolerate Our frequent reminders about battle. For them let it be not a battle, but the opening of the Gates. The process of opening also requires energy; but for you, without need of hypocritical palliation, it may be said that the battle of Light against darkness proceeds incessantly. Many warriors help in this battle, otherwise we again would be engulfed in Chaos. Often the participants in the battle ask why, in their physical shells, they do not remember the achievements of their subtle bodies. But it would be criminal on Our part to permit such consciousness. The heart could not bear the realization of so gigantic a battle. Only an especially flaming heart retains the black missiles in its consciousness. The heart is stopped, either because of realization or through sclerosis. But the cosmic battle can strike at the strongest heart.

Thus, let us remind about the battle, when the clash again assumes such colossal scope. The subterranean fire is equilibrated with difficulty, and the layers of magnetic currents are intercrossed. But let us not deny that this perturbation brings renewed possibilities.

355. The life-activity is intensified by different vibrations of the subtle energies. Thus the essence of life-activity and that upon which the life of each spirit is based are so inadequately realized. People think that the life process is contained only in the tissues, forgetting that the creativeness of Cosmos is intensified by the subtle energies and by that invisible process

which permits perpetual interchange and contact with the Spatial Fire. The maintenance of psychic energy is based upon the spiritual process. Verily, humanity must realize where is the source of life-activity and in what is contained the interchange for the growth of the forces. The moment humanity severed itself from the Source of Power, the shifting of the forces occurred; thus it is in the entire cosmic constructiveness.

Thus, in the entire structure the force is in need of saturation by the Source. Hence Hierarchy is so greatly stressed by Us, for this Source is the Source of Bliss, and in the epoch of the transformation of the world there is verily only one anchor of salvation. Therefore, consciousness should be affirmed upon the center of all that is given.

356. As the words imply, the evolutionary spiral expands and the involutionary spiral contracts. The very same may be observed not only in personal aspects but also in ideas. It is very instructive to discern how ideas are generated and how they complete their circle. Often they seem to disappear completely, but if they are of an evolutionary nature they appear again in an expanded form. For evolutionary thinking, one should study the spiral of the root of an idea. The task of the gradual containment of an idea can afford a progression toward a higher understanding. One may take for instance the idea of religions and examine it spirally; precisely, not comparatively, but evolutionally, spirally. Thus one can see the one root. Likewise one can study how the ideas of religions expanded through evolution. Thus, the prognosis of the future will not be diminished. Positive signs must be gathered.

357. Many concessions have been made by humanity in order to erase the vital foundation of the Teachings of Life. For the sake of comparative concessions

one may deprive the lamp of its wick and be astonished at the conflagration from the spilled oil.

The lamp of the world is overturned, and the sacred miracle of life can be safeguarded upon the mountains. The conflagration can be arrested by two fountainheads—Hierarchy and psychic energy.

358. Humanity must build its strongholds as a wondrous indivisible circle. Each creative inception must be built upon integrity and indivisibility, affirming itself in an orbit around the center. Only thus, by a radius, can one reach all points and establish the right scope. It should be understood that each stronghold must be nurtured from the center. The more superficial the receptivity, the more perilous it is in all directions. Therefore one should harken to the inner manifestation of the center. The indivisibility of the stronghold is its might. Integrity is its beauty. The center is the Hierarchy of Bliss. Thus the highest step is built. Each spirit must realize that all lives through the light of integrity. Each Ashram is nurtured by integrity and lives by the Light of Hierarchy. Each atom lives by integrity. In this is beauty; thus is the world constructed.

359. Our constructiveness lies in vitality. The pledge of happiness for humanity lies in beauty. Hence, We assert art to be the highest stimulus for the regeneration of the spirit. We consider art to be immortal and boundless. We make a demarcation between knowledge and science, because knowledge is art, science is method. Therefore, the element of Fire intensifies art and spirit-creativeness. Therefore, the wondrous pearls of art can actually uplift and transmute the spirit instantaneously. Everything is attainable through the growth of the spirit, for only the inner fires can give the needed strength of receptivity. Thus an Agni Yogi can sense all cosmic beauty without narrow scientific methodology. Verily, the pearls of art bring exaltation to humanity, and the fires of spirit-creativeness give a new understanding of beauty to humanity. Thus, We value integrity around the center and appreciate the Service to Hierarchy through the heart.

360. How pervertedly people interpret the foundations of the world! What formulas they invent for the interpretation of vital principles! Without understanding the great foundations of the unity of all cosmic principles, they saturate space with all the disrupting principles. Thus, there results imbalance of the origins, disunion of all the highest principles, and striving to many authorities. Thus, dividing the great Origin of Hierarchy through human frailty brings its effects, and humanity strains all efforts to depreciate the great Principle. Thus occurs the substitution of the small for the Great.

361. Verily, the cosmic Origins are wondrous in their might, and the creative law of Hierarchy imbues all with fire. Therefore, at the base of the entire Cosmos lies the law of the great unification of the highest fires. Hence all great designations should not be dissociated. And the foundation of the future, the radiant Hierarchy of Bliss, is indeed intensified in the assertion of great laws. Verily, it must be remembered that one can build only through Hierarchy. One may be in the orbit affirmed by Hierarchy only when the consciousness understands that a blow upon the Shield of the Name of the Hierarch is a blow at Us, and each one permitting a blow pays dearly. Thus, in unity lies the success of all works. The admittance of depreciation is an evidence of faint-heartedness and defection. Unity is a wondrous fire!

362. People are often more perturbed by thunder than by lightning. Likewise with events—people are more troubled by the reverberation than by the essence. One could say that there is no need to be terrified by thunder if the lightning has not struck! Only a novice fears the thunder of cannons and does not hear the flight of a bullet. Psychic energy reacts to the lightning. It can be seen how the natural capacities of the organism protect one from perilous conflagration. Thus psychic energy sometimes induces artificial swellings in order to divert a dangerous conflagration from an adjacent center. It is a very rare manifestation when, under one's eyes, the Yogi's extremities swell and the tissues as quickly contract to their former size. You witnessed such a manifestation when the center of the larynx was threatened by conflagration. In spite of the danger the psychic energy speedily mastered the fire.

Ejections likewise ward off inflammation; it is entirely analogous to volcanoes. A multitude of analogies are revealed to a searching eye. Only, one should not seek the artifice of a ritual, or forcing. The natural blending with the Highest is achieved only through a naturally kindled fire of the heart. Certainly the boiling of the Chalice that is filled to the brim is unavoidable, but this is the burden of the Mother of the World. Remember the ancient image of an infant lying in a chalice. A multitude of scientific signs are transformed into misty symbols, but it is time to study them.

363. During cosmic perturbations purifying fires are accumulated, which intensify the atmosphere and propel the fires for the construction of the New World. Thus, upon the ruins of the old world there rises a new evolution and the Epoch of Fire which terminates Kali Yuga and saturates space with the fire of the New World. Thus, the all-encompassing Banner of the Lords summons to pure creativeness. Thus the avowal of Hierarchy enters life. Thus, We welcome everything that is directed to Good. Thus, We welcome everything imbued with a pure striving to walk the higher path.

364. It is generally known that before the beginning of Satya Yuga the scroll of karma rolls up with especial rapidity. It may be asked why, then, many crimes and blasphemies remain seemingly unpunished? There are many reasons. The first, people prefer to judge by thunder rather than by lightning. The second, one may not notice how gradually the circle of events revolves. The third reason lies in the motive and in old karmic bonds. Thus, only a subtle consciousness can feel how, behind some undesirable action, there is concealed not a bad motive. But the reverse also happens when an action which is not apparently bad is the result of an inadmissible thought. When I speak of spatial justice, I have in mind the law of equilibrium. The Chalice will reflect each wavering of the spirit.

365. Observe how each deed reflects upon the fluctuation of karma. It can be perceived how treason in all its aspects calls forth a speedy formation of karma. One can learn much from such observations. How painful it is to see people harming themselves! It can be observed how thought, like a viper, strikes the inner being during these self-defeats. Nothing can avert the consequences, because cause and effect are too close. Thus, only by the fire of the heart can one defend oneself and purify the channel that carries infection.

366. How greatly people distort the concept of psychic powers, forgetting that a physical manifestation can always be explained by a psychic factor, but a psychic manifestation cannot be confirmed by physical means. When all psychic factors were eliminated from science then, certainly, a sharp demarcation between organic and inorganic occurred. Thus, one may point out to scholars that books bereft of spirit, psychic energy, and Cosmic Fire cannot produce the science that should be given to humanity. The separation of that which has existed for millenniums from that which was created through centuries has disclosed those errors which have precipitated so greatly the Karma of our planet.

Therefore, humanity must ponder on how to bring the psychic manifestations closer to the physical world. Otherwise, established science and pedantry may meet at an empty board. Therefore, the vitality of art, which guards the divine fire, gives to humanity the saturation by that fire which kindles the spirit and imbues all worlds. Hence, the wondrous torches of the beauty of creativeness are so precious for humanity. We have seen how the creations of art have transformed men—something all the book-learning in the world cannot do. Thus the Banner of Beauty and Peace unites the world. Thus spirit-creativeness saturates space.

367. Who is the giver? The one who possesses. But lest one become exhausted one should receive from the inexhaustible Source. Let us turn toward Hierarchy.

368. You have heard of the fragrance emanating from the saints. We shall point out how the aura of saints, bringing them back to the bloodless kingdom, gives them the fragrance of the flowers through which they passed during their round of early incarnations. Thus, one can also heal by applying corresponding flowers to the body.

369. When spiritual quests involve millenniums how can one deny their achievements? What errors occur on the ground of denial of fiery achievements! Thus it can be affirmed that invisible processes reveal the power of action to humanity. Thus, one should understand that spiritual energy is the element of Cosmic Fire, which moves life and imbues all vital manifestations. The power of knowledge of the highest energies is the key to Be-ness. The signs of psychic energy are spatially diffused in the entire Universe; therefore one should harken to the Spatial Fire.

370. One of the most harmful actions is the condemnation of Hierarchy for the consequences of our own mistakes. Except treason, nothing so definitely severs the link with the Hierarchy as does such ignorant condemnation. The protecting veil of Hierarchy minimizes in everything the consequences of harmful mistakes, but to reject Hierarchy means to bring upon oneself the entire torrent of consequences. One experienced sailor advised, "Never change ships during a storm." One may remember how people, having committed an error, often have tried to explain its consequences as a sacrifice to Hierarchy, not realizing that by this they have already condemned Hierarchy.

371. The adherence to Fire affords saturation of the centers by the cosmic rhythm. Hence, the resonance is affirmed by a continuous adherence to the spatial current. The sensitiveness of the centers must be protected and affirmed as a bond between the visible and invisible worlds. During the resonance of the centers, quiet should be observed.

372. The affirmation of the Teacher should be repeated each hour, for Our structure is in need of a conscious adoption of Hierarchy. Various events may be expected, but participation in them can only be through the Hierarchy proclaimed by Us. Thus I say, Not only Our decision but the karma of millenniums makes the structure of the future immutable. Details may be changed, but the foundation must not be violated. Thus, Our Will should not be forgotten, even in the details of life. You realize correctly the creative fairy tale, but only upon the ladder of Hierarchy

will it be transformed into the salvation of the world. Thus I speak.

373. "Labor, create good, reverence the Hierarchy of Light"—this, Our Commandment, can be inscribed even upon the palm of a newly born child. Thus simple is the Commandment leading to Light. In order to adopt it one must only be pure in heart.

374. When the planet loses its equilibrium owing to the loss of spiritual understanding, the consequences to the planet are inevitable; for there is no karmic effect without cause and no cause without effect. The manifestation called forth by the loss of spiritual strivings will certainly induce those impulses which will bring regeneration to the planet. The appearance of physical changes will give to the planet the understanding of Agni Yoga. The financial crash will effect a revaluation of values. The distortion of religions will result in a search for a new spiritual achievement.

Therefore, verily, the crumbling of the old world is a new affirmation, for through the coming of new values We bring to the world the salvation of spirit.

375. Thus, upon the principle of Fire the world is regenerated. The fire of the centers, the fire of the spirit, the fire of the heart, the fire of achievement, the fire of attainment, the fire of Hierarchy, the fire of Service—these constitute the principles of the New World. The blended arcs of consciousnesses thus create the Highest Will. Verily, the great Banner of Peace will cover the entire world. Verily, a great time, the time of great fulfillments. Thus the time of great action approaches.

376. I shall say of treason to the fanatics and bigots. They assume that treason is only a matter of thirty pieces of silver, but they forget that it is contained in each blasphemy and slander. One should not think that a malicious word is not also treason. It is precisely malice that is often inseparable from treason and slander. One and the same black tree nurtures these loathsome branches, and their fruits are as black as the roots of shame. One must speedily liberate oneself from the horror of malicious words.

377. The transformation of the world is indeed affirmed in the highest tension. All perturbations, all shiftings, all diseases accompany this transformation. The most powerfully propelled energies bring fires into motion. Thus, in the Epoch of Fire darkness becomes dense, and everything is intensified in a fiery striving. Evil is created by the densified darkness. Light transforms the world. Thus, at the great time, the manifestation of the universal transmutation saturates space.

Thus, during the Epoch of Fire, when Light battles with darkness, the manifestation of the Banner of Peace is that fundamental sign which will give a new step to humanity. Thus Beauty, Knowledge, Art, and all nations will unite under this sign. Thus, only the highest measures can be applied to the Banner. Verily!

378. Resistance to evil is one of the fundamental qualities of those who are in search of Hierarchy. Physical qualities will not give tenacity against evil, but the spirit and the fire of the heart will create an armor against the cunning of evil. But how to understand evil? Certainly, first of all, it is destruction. But replacing an old house with a new and better one will not be destruction. By destruction is meant dissolution leading to an amorphous state. One must know how to oppose such destruction. One should find the strength of spirit to overcome the cowardice inherent in non-resistance. Thus let there be readiness to oppose evil.

379. How greatly must consciousness be expanded in order to comprise all broad affirmations and to

understand the entire task. Correspondence, co-measurement, and tension should be realized, for without this understanding one can diminish a world task by measuring it in small dimensions. Thus, when creating an urgent world step, first of all, a world scale must be applied. Thus, when the great Banner, the sign of the New Epoch, is unfurled, conscious measures should be applied. Therefore, the great proclamation must be understood as a step toward the regeneration of the world.

380. Are there not enough earthquakes? Are there not enough wrecks, storms, excesses of cold and heat? Has not the fiery cross risen? Has not a star shone by day? Has not a fiery rainbow flared? Have not the signs sufficiently multiplied? But humanity amidst chaos does not wish to be aware of the apparent signs! And so We shall not insist upon a visible sign when doubt has blinded the people. But amidst these blind and deaf the children of fire are found. To them We send signs, that they shall know of the approach of Light.

381. The consciousness that encompasses only the present, without any thought of the future, cannot adhere to evolution, because the chain of centuries disappears for such a consciousness. Hence, when the consciousness expands it encompasses the great leading chain of causes and effects. Thus, while evolution is being established, the manifestation of causes is so important. At present, when the planet is completing its Karma, certainly the retribution for engenderments is greatly reflected upon humanity. Yet that which is engendered by human spiritual striving enwraps the planet. Hence each bright tension and striving will give to the planet the affirmation of the New World. Therefore, the lofty Banner of Peace carries its projectiles of Light and fierily imbues the currents around

Earth as a panacea against evil. The consciousnesses blended for millenniums create. Thus Light conquers darkness. Thus a wondrous step is being fulfilled. Thus the preordained approaches.

382. Cosmic justice resolves all karmic ties. And how little humanity ponders upon the affirmations that bear us through space! Would they but ponder upon the affirmations that carry us into the higher spheres, they would invariably arrive at Hierarchy. Thus humanity would garb itself in the realization of Truth. Thus, upon the blending of the arcs of consciousnesses We create the future.

383. If even radio waves react so powerfully upon man, how powerfully can objects saturated with psychic energy act! The magnet that is consciously saturated transmits its magnetic currents; thus Our emanations surround each transmitted gift. Therefore the affirmed action of Our sendings can always intensify the strength of the one to whom they are sent. Space is raging. Perturbations are accumulating, but above all events a new current is directed for the step of regeneration.

384. Can anyone assert that Our Guidance has belittled him? Can anyone say that We have destroyed his best structures? Can anyone find in Our Guidance destruction and disparagement? No! The heart of each one will say that even mistakes have been erased, if one's own apostasy did not impede. You could testify how the apostates harmed themselves, but of these consequences they themselves were guilty. It is glorious to lead the pure soul, unstained by apostasy, along the summits of Be-ness. The affinity is evidenced as the consequence of cooperation. We call to such cooperation, which binds forever.

385. Cosmic magnetism imbues every vital process. Our task is to establish the physical correlation of vibrations, for thus it will be possible to determine the correlations of all manifestations. Each manifestation is linked with the centers of subtle energies. Each flash, each vibration, is correlated with a certain manifestation in Cosmos. Studying these waves, one may come to the conclusion that the bond between all manifestations is so powerful that by it one may determine where lies the link with magnetism; thus, different thoughts, standards, and aspirations are impeded by magnetism of different tensions.

386. Only the unexpected terrifies and frightens. Everything anticipated already enters into life. This means that the unexpected should be transformed into the expected. In other words one should strive to knowledge. Furthermore, this knowledge should be understood, not formally, but in its entire multiformity. When the might of life itself shall imbue us with its endless variety, the vanguard under the three spheres will be invincible. But cognizance of the three spheres should be achieved, or else we shall move only along the surface. You must hasten to accustom yourself to the necessity of movement, within your inner cognizance. The Teaching will not guide one if it is not applied.

387. In the development of the works hostility will certainly be encountered, but one must firmly remember two conditions: the first—hostile people should be avoided, because they are not predestined; the second—perhaps just this hostility will serve as a worthy springboard. But delay is not caused by enemies—look closer!

388. When a victory was announced to the emperor known to you, he accepted this message in complete calm. The courtiers whispered, "Is it indifference?" But the sovereign said, "Not indifference, but knowledge. For me this victory is already passed, and at present I am thinking of a great difficulty."

When We say guard your health, or do not give your writings into alien hands, or do not leave your home, We have foreseen many circumstances already transpired, which should have been avoided. Who else, then, can define the consequences so solicitously as We, as the Teacher? When We speak of gratitude it is certainly not because We are in need of it, but by this We try to strengthen the bond once more. Each disunity is as perilous as a hook with bait in the hands of the fisherman.

389. The dark forces attempt to battle with Light. They try to affirm their dark deeds, strengthening themselves by treason, but the Forces of Light are greatly strained and bestow so many manifestations necessary for creation! The shifting of forces is strained by the dark counteraction. Thus, Hierarchy faces all tension in the name of the great creation. Hierarchy bears the plan for the shifting. Thus, evolution advances powerfully.

390. How stupid are all who deny hope! How blind are those who affirm the advantage of wars! How few are the consciousnesses that can perceive the regeneration of the planet by way of culture! Certainly, those who do not comprehend creativeness by means of higher measures will perish in the same old upheavals. Those who do not comprehend the new ways are greatly in need of understanding the Epoch of Maitreya. The Banner of Peace and of the Lords will open all ways!

391. Again they will come to you in doubt about the law of karma. "Is it possible that the unfit ones can revel in comfort, whereas worthy ones suffer?" Answer,

"Heavy is the karma of those who cannot forego earthly comfort, for it is said, 'Comfort is the cemetery of the spirit.' " Besides, as you have observed, earthly comfort shuts out spiritual hearing. But many, under the mask of well-being, hide the greatest misfortunes. Therefore none of those who know will apply the standards of earthly comfort. One should judge according to the summits, not thinking of subterranean torrents.

392. The Teacher is glad to see how you become accustomed to understanding the possibility of difficulties. One should become accustomed to this blessed realization. It is one of the first conditions of adherence to the Hierarchy.

Sometimes I advise you to be silent; also, one must realize the significance of tension of space caused by a conscious silence. Moreover, one must remind about the rhythm of repetitions. It is unwise to overlook the help of technique and of various conditions. Take, for instance, the condition of a headache. What could be better than silence? Or during palpitations of the heart, the cosmic rhythm, which changes the pulse?

393. Service is often taken as an affirmation quite opposed to Truth. Service is regarded as something not conforming to reality. Service is regarded as a ritual, as a rhythm, which entered life incidentally. But it must be realized that Service is a chain which connects the Higher with the lower, and is affirmed in life and preordained by the manifested essence; thus the entire chain of Service enters into the Hierarchy of Bliss. Thus all actions form a unifying chain; hence the law of Hierarchy can bring us to the Highest Bliss.

394. The intensification of energy between the disciple and Teacher is analogous to a steam engine—a continuous projection and restitution. Therefore We point out so persistently the necessity of concordance, for benevolence, striving, and gratitude. Only by those means can one develop the dynamics of concordance. A steam engine is provided with fuel, but We have an inexhaustible reservoir of psychic energy. One should not think that the enumerated qualities are needed by Us; on the contrary they are needed by you. Otherwise how will you strengthen the bond with Us? The powerful rhythm of the dynamo of spirit can be affirmed, not by doubt, egoism or self-pity, but only by an indivisible, vigorous striving toward Us. These strivings must be introduced into life. It should be remembered that each physical law must remind of the stability of the laws of the spirit. With such a consciousness one can verily become a co-worker for the transformation of life.

395. Humanity has sunk in the mire of outworn survivals, in old thoughts, beyond the realization of affirmed Existence. Thus the spirit of the shifted nations smolders under the departing energies of bigotry and superstition. The basis of this smoldering—the church that sows terror—is intolerable. A state that acts by means of treason cannot live. Thus, the regeneration of the spirit must eliminate these horrors which engulf the planet. Hence, only the Chain of Hierarchy can restore the human image. Thus, a new affirmation is being built by means of eternal Hierarchy.

396. When the world is convulsed and humanity heaves in turmoil, there remains only one path to salvation. How is it possible not to realize the highest, and the creative, path of the ascent of the spirit! Just now when all the old ways are destroyed, when all the old energies are out-lived, when the planet itself shifts its crust, how is it possible not to adopt with one's entire spirit the new affirmations and the regenerating energies emanating from the might of the Chain of Hierarchy! Only thus can humanity be attracted to the higher energies. Following the foundations of the Cosmic Magnet, the highest manifestation will attract the spirit to the Highest. Thus, the highest law of Hierarchy creates through beneficence, affirming a better future.

397. During a trance, even the most average man becomes adroit, daring, indefatigable, begins to learn much of what is as yet inaccessible to him, and the evidence of the invisible world becomes apparent to him, merely because for a time he has parted from the lower physical world. But on returning to it the man forgets his higher substance as though it were a dream. A bridge must be found to prevent the loss of consciousness and to become enriched by the Higher World. Agni Yoga is given to bring people to the Higher World.

They will say, Why the pains of a Yogi? Certainly this is the burden of this world. Pains are unnecessary where the cosmic rhythm is not violated. Therefore it is beneficial for a Yogi to have a better attuned circle around him in order to give a certain form to the approaching cosmic waves. Therefore, when I speak of harmony, I do not have in mind only sensitiveness; I point out a useful construction. Hierarchy stands upon exact laws. We, who have realized them, take upon Ourselves the responsibility of protecting this ladder of Light. One must repeat this untiringly in order that the structure of Hierarchy may be impressed as a design upon the brain.

398. The accumulations of cosmic energies correspond to the affirmations of human disturbances of spirit. During such cosmic correspondence the disturbances can be resolved only by such a powerful lever as Hierarchy. When the chain of events destroys the

old foundations, saturating space with tossing energies, then certainly a force is needed that can propel all energies to new constructiveness. Hierarchy is the link that transforms the departing energies into a radiant future. To the world, Hierarchy is the affirmation of a cosmic dimension. In Cosmos everything is bound by the affirmed dimensions of a powerful Hierarchy. Thus, all energies are mutually bound. Thus, the thread of the heart is linked with Hierarchy. Thus, this great bond establishes the cosmic Substance.

399. When a new race is assembled, the Assembler is a Hierarch. When a new step for humanity is built, the Builder is a Hierarch. When the step preordained by the Cosmic Magnet is constructed upon the vital rhythm, a Hierarch stands at its head. There is no manifestation of life which does not contain in its seed its Hierarch. The more powerful the step, the more powerful the Hierarch.

400. Compared to the vegetable kingdom, the animal kingdom provides far more feasible experiments. If one understood Agni Yoga, one could feel to what an extent the influence of man exerts itself on animals. It can be seen to what an extent irritation or fear or assurance is transmitted to them. Certainly the law of Yogism extends from a "deadly eye" to resurrection. But through a multitude of intermediate steps one may observe various effects. Those who approach Agni Yoga should be warned of the possible consequences of thoughtless actions. How many unpleasantnesses might be avoided by simple self-discipline, to which one should accustom oneself. How many achievements accumulated through centuries are swept away by an unrestrained roaring. One must think of self-perfectment. One must arouse in oneself the superiority of the spirit, which will always be sustained by Hierarchy.

401. The superiority of the spirit will not come if we do not strive toward it. One must assimilate the thought about the transitoriness of the earthly hour and the immutability of the Infinite. Thus Agni Yoga is linked inseparably with Infinity and Hierarchy. Likewise, one can transport oneself to the microcosm of the heart, which contains the reflexes of the far-off worlds. How enticing it is to understand within oneself the rhythms that guide the planet! Certainly, at the time of disturbances it is difficult, but how wondrous it is to adhere to the Cosmic Magnet.

402. All cosmic disturbances are reflected upon and mutually intensified by vital manifestations. Each energy corresponds to a vital manifestation. Thus when the imbalance and destruction of all the old foundations are affirmed on the planet, the subterranean fire, whirlwinds, and physical destruction of the crust are powerfully intensified. When the fiery sign of Hierarchy is being affirmed on the planet, conditions are indeed intensified by the vivifying fire. Thus, the great affirmation is asserted by the highest fire of the life of Hierarchy.

403. Can you indicate any disparagement in the Decrees of the Teacher? You cannot, for then the Teacher would not be worthy of this title. But can you vouch for your own actions, since disparaging is contrary to the Brotherhood? Disparagement is involution, whereas upliftment is evolution. We serve evolution. One can find Commands, warnings, and even indignation, but there is no disparagement in Our Works. Even Our adversaries are not belittled. Two types of people differ especially—some will create something great, even out of a small hint; others will create a repulsive image, even out of a beautiful vision. Each one judges according to his consciousness. One is great in heart; the other has a heart like a dried mushroom, which one must soak in water before it is of use. Verily, one must redeem all mistakes. Remember this law.

404. It is said that the shirt on a traitor burns. One can notice how things are ruined in the proximity of a sick psychic energy.

405. When the centers are fierily intensified, it means that correspondence with the cosmic perturbations should be found. The signs are accurate and ascertained by close bonds between Cosmos and an Agni Yogi. Thus the bond reveals concordance with all currents of space. Thus a striving Agni Yogi displays a responsive vibration to all fiery manifestations. Therefore, health must be guarded. A very important time; space vibrates and the whirlwinds are powerful.

406. A traveler is in need of indications. Success is a very sensitive flower. The seeds can be planted only at a designated time. One must leave the house in time. But when the Teacher ordains the sowing, not a moment should be lost. Only children can think that if today has passed, tomorrow will be better. But a courageous mind understands that success that is missed will not be repeated. Even the sun does not shine uniformly. Refinement of understanding should be developed. The complexity of the time will increase. He who did not discriminate yesterday will not be resourceful tomorrow. The Teacher foresees an undeferrable, immediate sowing.

407. A hurricane may bring heaps of gold ashore; human turmoil can likewise yield treasures. One must remember that turmoil intensifies energies. The Teacher is on vigil. The Teacher observes the imperceptible functions. He knows who will discriminate and who will be able to receive the gifts.

408. The kings of spirit—where are they? Often people place themselves on the level of a king of spirit, forgetting that the most essential quality of a king of spirit is his following of a Hierarch. Can one ascend to the level of a king of spirit by neglecting the Hierarch? Can one expect esteem for oneself through disparaging the Hierarch? Do not those who oppose the Hierarch carry ineradicable stains on themselves? Thus, let humanity remember and ponder upon how to become true kings of spirit! Thus, one may warn those who wish to become kings of spirit. Not by self-glorification do we reach the kingly step of spirit. Not by striving to an evident self-doom can one reach the affirmation of the step of a king of the spirit.

Therefore, We advise each one to follow a Hierarch.

409. Thus, We have a list of those following a Hierarch, those denying a Hierarch, and those who openly oppose the Most High. Certainly the life of each one who, if only a few times, opposes a Hierarch, becomes very complicated, because such is the law of life. Hence it must be realized how important it is to follow a Hierarch. Thus, the important time must be attested. Thus, one should have an understanding of the manifested time. Thus, We attest the New World. Indeed, the dark ones are infuriated and frightened, but We are more powerful than darkness. Thus, all dugpas condemn themselves to annihilation.

410. Again the deniers of Hierarchy will come and term it leadership by coercion. Again you will tell them, "Hierarchy has nothing in common with coercion. It is the revealing law which discloses." We oppose any coercion. We do not direct the energy without the consent of the co-worker. We know the worthlessness of everything superficial and outwardly propelled. Like a builder, We summon co-workers. But We leave him, who is not in need of Our boat, to cross the ocean even if it be on a bamboo stick. Yet people often are so fearful of all cooperation that they are ready to plunge into mud rather than contact the Highest. Many times you will have to sunder yourself from people on account of Hierarchy. They would rather accept Infinity, because they do not feel their responsibility before it. Furthermore, the unavoidableness of the law of Hierarchy disturbs the limited, selfish mind.

Learn not to insist where you see that the path is besmirched. One cannot go against karma. But a multitude of foolish ones have sinned against Hierarchy, hence the froth of their irritation.

411. When the world is plunged into the darkness of denial, then indeed, one must expect the destruction of old unfit foundations, for how else can the world be regenerated? How can humanity come to its senses if not by the shattering of all unfit foundations? Only when the new and affirmed great principles of Hierarchy are realized by humanity will it be possible to confirm humanity's salvation. Thus, We intensely impel the planet to the principles of the Hierarchy of Good. The loss of the highest concepts must be compensated for, because each lost principle brings cosmic upheavals. Thus, humanity must be regenerated upon the principle of Hierarchy.

412. Only by renewal of thinking can humanity attain the new planetary step. What a spatial tension surrounds the planet! Such ominous forebodings have taken place only before a stupendous cosmic conflict. Therefore, only when Our Hierarchy shall be affirmed can humanity be saved.

413. The contemporary dugpas do not find labor too difficult. One has only to say, "How beautiful you are," and the fruit will fall. But if one slackens, then dugpa will tenderly advise, "Defer." Thus, he will find a moment when the man lays aside his strength and possibilities. Certainly, a third and most beloved expedient still remains—precisely gold.

We protect only those upon the right path. When someone wavers in darkness, he falls out of the area of the Ray.

414. What thorns people weave into their wreaths of life! What strength people dissipate to counteract those principles upon which life itself is maintained! How many unnecessary thorns surround people, transforming their lives into regress! People will not understand the higher Wisdom if they do not first of all understand the law of Hierarchy—that upon which the entire life is founded; that by which the world progresses; that upon which evolution is built; that upon which the best steps and pages of history have been constructed. Thus, humanity cannot evade the great law of Hierarchy. Self-destruction is the only direction along which those bereft of the understanding of Hierarchy proceed; thus, the thorns directed against Hierarchy turn into a dark path. Thus, the great law of Hierarchy must be safeguarded as a leading principle.

415. In the small and in the great, one must be imbued with the guiding law of Hierarchy. Thus only will one be able to build the great future. Upon the blending of the arcs of consciousnesses is life built. Hierarchy and leadership are affirmed upon the cosmic law. Hence creativeness of spirit is so essentially imbued with the Cosmic Magnet. Thus, the leader is in contact with the Cosmic Magnet, and the entire saturation of the world can be intensified by this great law. Thus We create through the merging of consciousness and heart.

416. Hierarchy is a goal-fitting cooperation—thus

this part of the Teaching can be termed. But let us not be concerned if you use the old Greek word Hierarchy. If someone interprets it according to the conventional understanding, he will only prove that his brain is not yet ready for cooperation.

417. Each spirit creates its own karma. Each nation builds its own Karma. Certainly nations are looking for a leader, because even an established prestige cannot sustain those people who think erroneously. Neither gold nor vulgar, glamorous names, nor piles of inapplicable counsels will save a nation. Verily, the fiery thought, the fiery spirit of the leader will provide new ways. Therefore, let the star of the Spiritual Leader shine brightly at the time of cosmic perturbations. Thus, let the great Realm of Light rise upon the ruins of the old world.

Thus, the attraction has been manifested as a great Might. Thus, the time of the great predestined New World has come. Therefore, woe to those who go against Hierarchy!

418. Diseases are divided as sacred, karmic, and those that are admitted. The first two concepts are easily understood, but precisely in the book Hierarchy one should mention the admitted ones. Who or what permits these diseases? Certainly ignorance and the horror of non-realization. It is not enough not to think about them. Children likewise do not think of them, yet become infected. One should protect oneself in consciousness and create an invulnerable armor of nerve emanations. Even severe epidemics cannot develop if people master their consciousnesses. An experiment with the substance of psychic energy would indicate what powerful antiseptics people carry within themselves. For this, two conditions are necessary: the first—realization of psychic energy; the second—realization of Hierarchy as the sole path for the increase of psychic energy. One should not look upon Hierarchy as something abstract. One should realize firmly that it is the most powerful life-giver. We call it the primary remedy. But even a pill must be swallowed and an ointment applied. There is no effect from a remedy that is in a trunk. Likewise, the Benefaction of Hierarchy must be taken by striving. Thus, an irrevocable striving will afford a healing result.

419. You have witnessed many magic methods, and finally you have come to the understanding of the magnet of the heart and to the realization of psychic energy. Indeed, why is a substitute needed if one can receive the might of the Source itself? Many accumulations are accepted by humanity instead of striving to the Higher World. People presume that it is easier to reiterate the unrealized formulas than to cognize that which is the closest to the human essence. Striving upward is not natural to men when the spirit suffers. But is it not better to substitute higher striving for suffering?

420. Illumination of the spirit! How can one reach this step? How can one penetrate into the primary source of Truth, if not by adhering to Hierarchy? The spirit can be illumined only through the source of Light. Where can one find a leading ray, if not in Hierarchy? Humanity has been drawing its power, not from within itself, but from the power of the great Hierarchy. Thus through centuries Our creativeness has guided humanity. Thus man can be directed only by the Higher Power of Hierarchy. The illumination of the spirit is assuredly the path of adherence to the highest Hierarchy. Hence, those who search for Truth can find the significance of Be-ness only in the path of ascent toward Hierarchy, otherwise life remains a vicious circle, and for millenniums the spirit will not find its liberation. Thus, the law of Hierarchy is the leading principle.

421. The spirit cannot be affirmed and display its strength without drawing its power from Hierarchy. The spirit cannot manifest power without adopting the Higher Power; therefore each creator of life is a link in the great Hierarchy. Thus, also Our Guidance is the great Regency.

422. If you know that an exalted, self-denying thought physically changes one's aura and even induces rays from the shoulders, then you already know one of the great mysteries of the world. Each visibility is the reflex of a material reaction. Thus, if irritation generates imperil, then each exalted thought must create an opposite beneficial substance. And so it is. Certainly Bliss is a complete reality. It is generated in the cortical system and reacts upon the brain matter. The Tibetan ringse has a deep significance, being the sediment crystallized by the manifestation of Bliss. Certainly it is difficult to investigate the substance of Bliss while alive, for the heart and brain cannot be touched. The manifestation of imperil is much easier to approach, in the nerve channels of the extremities. But at the same time it would be unjust to disclose to humanity the negative substance and to presuppose only theoretically the existence of the most salutary substance. Of course, in the laboratory which is being created both substances will be demonstrated. We shall not assist the usual experiments, but where the steps of evolution are being built Our Hand will be on guard! First, We shall give attention to establishing the fact of imperil. Afterward, We shall define the ways of the manifestation of Bliss. If ancient science preserved fragmentary memories about the sediments of Bliss, then, certainly a biochemist can show more contemporary proofs of it. Later, these experiments upon the substance of the organism will be transferred to spatial energies. And again we shall understand why Bliss has the closest correlation to Hierarchy.

423. Indeed, it is not necessary to call forth irritation, because men are filled to the brim with it. It is only necessary to lock six bipeds in one room and within an hour the door will be shaking from imperil. It is more difficult with Bliss, but here, also, the knowledge of Agni Yoga and close cooperation with certain plants will provide a perceptible result. Certainly the densification of the astral body will provide irreplaceable possibilities. A difficult time affords new approaches, and the tread of the New World is already audible.

424. Roses are beneficial for Bliss. All helpful means should be assembled. Not without reason was the rose the symbol of mystery in alchemy. But nowadays rose oil is very poorly prepared.

425. Verily inscrutable are Our ways! To the ignorant it seems that the invisible world does not exist; they show prejudice against everything not perceptible to their coarse senses. Truly, since man cannot accept the sacred ways, how will he understand the highest and limitless foundation of life? Man must realize and feel all the subtle sensations; without this, there can be no correspondence and affirmation evidenced by the understanding of Hierarchy.

426. Faith is the presentiment of knowledge. In the multiformity of the All-Existent, faith has an actual foundation. Like a motive force, faith intensifies the energy and through this increases the working capability of space. One can welcome the tensity of energy when it is connected with the manifestation of the substance of Bliss. Thus We can point out the most evi-

dent path of faith together with an uplifted and refined consciousness. Certainly, Hierarchy is that megaphone which will stir the heavens to thunder.

427. Despair is the death of faith. But faith is knowledge. Therefore despair is the death of knowledge, the death of all accumulations. Despair is always connected with a feeling of issuelessness. The usual method of the dark ones is to confine their victim in a circle without issue and then urge him to crime. Indeed, where can the victim turn if he is not aware of the path upward? For those who know the Bliss of Hierarchy there can be no such thing as issuelessness and despair. Thus, one can trace to what an extent the Teaching has in mind an essential, direct benefit, which can be given to everyone who knows how to look upward.

428. One must learn to address oneself to Hierarchy as the most immutable. What power the invocation of Hierarchy can give one, without waste and wavering! But these waverings, though swifter than a heartbeat, can sting the consciousness worse than a deadly viper. One must accustom oneself to constant communion with Hierarchy. Only thus is the nest of life built in the heart.

429. The earthly life span cannot be lived through without Hierarchy. But the difference lies in the kind of hierarchy that can be comprised by the consciousness. In disintegration one can turn to the hierarchy of gold and even to the hierarchy of gluttony.

430. How much significance people attribute to their ego! How people dread that their personality may be intruded upon by something incomprehensible to their consciousness! How people dread to adhere to the Highest and prefer to remain on the boundary of darkness! Each intention brings one closer to a bet-

ter decision if the spirit strives toward the Hierarchy of Bliss. Man can ascend each step in evolution if he accepts the Leading Hand and each Command of Hierarchy. History is built by the Hierarchy of life. The best steps of humanity were built by Hierarchy. The best achievements were affirmed by Hierarchy. Thus one can attain only through Hierarchy.

Thus is the Great Time affirmed, and We saturate space with a lofty call.

431. A sensitive heart is close to the sensitive ear. A sensitive heart transforms the brain. The lack of heart annihilates all previous accumulations. What is the use of literacy if only superficial eyes measure the curves of a hieroglyph! Onerous is the Burden of the World! Filled to the brim is the Chalice of the Keepers of the Magnet! Flaming hearts can combat everywhere the annihilation of the essence of Bliss. One can comprehend why one should become accustomed to understanding the heart as the propellant of Be-ness. One can understand how the thread of the heart is linked with Hierarchy. If the heart is withered the brain will not be kindled to consciousness. Thus we realize chemically how an organism becomes part of the great Heart of the Universe. When I advise cautiousness it means that outer conditions set the overfilled Chalice atremor.

432. How, then, does humanity hope to save its Karma and advance its evolution? Certainly not by denial of the great foundations, not through disparaging the highest principles, not by destruction of the affirmed and manifested Origins! Still, humanity continues to base its principles upon destruction, not realizing that breaking away from the great Hierarchy carries it to the abyss. Thus, self-destruction is the fate of all servitors of darkness. Thus, as long as humanity

directs itself to the limitations established by darkness it will not find the path to the Highest Light and salvation.

433. What state flourishes without a great leader? What affirmed undertaking has existed without a leader? Verily one must understand that the concept of a leader is the synthesis of all the highest strivings. Thus, only the concept of Hierarchy, of an Illumined Leader, can direct the spirit. Thus, let all, all, all ponder upon and remember the Might of Hierarchy. Only through this realization can one advance. Only through this realization can one attain. Let it be remembered that each stone thrown at Hierarchy will be transformed into a mountain against oneself. Thus let all remember! Thus We proclaim the Leader—the Hierarch!

434. Help each other, harken! Help in the small and in the great. Help is a rap upon the future. You know not which is the drop that filled the cup to the brim. I shall remind you of a tale of ancient India: King Rishiputra could no longer sleep. He summoned a Sage to restore his sleep to him. The Sage said, "King, examine thy couch." The royal couch was examined, and a stone was found in the folds of the sheets. The King rejoiced, believing that this was the cause of his affliction. But sleep did not return and the Sage repeated his advice. Again the couch was examined, and a dead butterfly was found. Again the King was sure that the cause of his sleeplessness was discovered. But his sleep did not return. The Sage said, "There is no effect without cause. Thou thyself, King, examine thy couch; for nothing can take the place of one's own eye." And the King found under his pillow a grain of gold, small as a mustard seed. "This minute grain could not have harmed me," thought the King. But sleep immediately closed his eyes. In the morning the Sage pointed out to the King, "The downfall of the spirit is not measured by fourths. The treasures of war cannot outweigh a seed taken from a widow. Help, King, wherever help can reach."

Help wherever the hand can reach, wherever a thought can fly. Thus shall we rap upon the future. Hence, let us remember that each hour taken from oneself will be recorded for the future. One must become accustomed to the fact that Our cooperation brings all that is needed if the hand that holds the current does not wither.

The heart aflame with help is Our heart. Thus we may face the time which is terrible for the ignorant, but bright for the knowing.

435. When will humanity learn to understand wherein consists the true dignity of a nation? When will humanity understand that the sacred spirit should be protected, and that the carriers of thought, as the sole source, can guide nations? Thus, through the annihilation of thought one may deprive a nation of its strength or of the predestined influence. Hence each nation should take care of its Pilot first of all, since the boat without a rudder cannot withstand the storm. Therefore, the great care of a nation and of each construction must be founded upon Hierarchy; for each structure must be saturated by the power from Above. Thus, as long as the understanding of Hierarchy is not affirmed, humanity will sink in the ignorance and darkness of destruction.

This is why the dark ones are on watch, for they sense how powerfully the world searches for and is in need of reconstruction—thus the dark ones affirm their own ruin!

436. Let no one think that without the energies of

the heart he can comprehend help, cooperation, and Hierarchy. Neither the mind nor intellectual erudition will enlighten where only the tensity of the heart can kindle the rainbow of complete comprehension. The shield of heart-comprehension is most lasting. The sword pierces suffering, but the heart is the stronghold of the hero. To you, the keepers of the Stone, only heroism is befitting. Only unwaveringness and courage befit you. The ecstasy of a hero comes again with the tension of the heart.

437. Truly, in the days of perturbations there exists only one salvation for humanity. Thought that leads to the understanding of Hierarchy is the only way by which humanity can be brought to the goal of realization of the highest affirmed Hierarchy. Thus, in the days of chaos one can say that only by following the Hierarchy can one reach the best step, for the leadership of the spirit is the all-comprising and all-encompassing might. Thus it can be asserted when the Cosmic Magnet transmits its might to humanity through the leadership of the spirit. Therefore, one should adopt progress through Hierarchy as the salvation of the planet.

438. Even the imagination is created by a lengthy experience of accumulations through the centuries, and all qualities of the spirit pertain to the same law. The quality of heroism must also be created and tempered in life. We do not casually remind you of the days of past heroism, at the hour when the firmness of the spirit must again be evidenced. We remind of how soon the valiant and invincible heroism must be manifested. Thus the accumulations of the spirit are awakened. How, then, can the realization of the beauty of heroism be created if it has not been justified by experience in life? How, then, can one affirm that heroism is beautiful, if the spirit remembers not the transport of the rays of achievement? What, then, can lift us above the chaos of mediocrity if not the wings of achievement? Thus, it is best when Hierarchy can evoke a spark of the very same feelings which formerly strengthened and uplifted the spirit.

439. One should gather the armor of the spirit when the earth is atremor. Can the mountains be in dread and trees be in terror? Certainly they can, if their spirit is in contact with the developed consciousness of man. But can the lake rejoice and the flowers be merry? Certainly they can, if flowers even wither under the glance of man. Such is the correlation between the lowest and highest links of Hierarchy. Only a very refined spirit will find within himself the courage to acknowledge a brother even in a rock.

440. Great firmness, great determination must be evidenced when the goal is communion with Us. But even a minor treason generates numerous calamities. I warn those who have ears.

441. In the mighty shifting of nations what can be the saving manifestation? What else can provide the direction to the Good if not the way toward Hierarchy? When the spirit of humanity sinks into the lower strata, what can bring it to the higher understanding if not adherence to Hierarchy? The Epoch of Fire approaches, which will bring to humanity great attainments and equally great transmutations, because the Epoch of Fire can be assimilated by the spirit that adheres to Hierarchy.

Our co-workers must therefore understand that only through fiery striving can one attain. In the Epoch of Fire one can build only by fire. Each indifference, each delay, each display of egoism is the manifestation of ruin. But the disparagement of Hierarchy is most heinous of all.

442. If you want to ponder upon the Three Pearls of the World, can you feel your heart as a summit, bestowing power upon the three sacred rivers, which nurture many lands? Can you master the trinity of consciousness without diminishing one part? The spirit must be accustomed to divisibility. One can imagine amidst sloping hills a strong snowy summit, which takes upon itself all the burden of the whirlwinds. So rises an Arhat, who takes upon himself the entire burden of imperfection. As clouds hover around the summit, sometimes screening it from earthly eyes, so the wearisome burdens of the world pierce the Chalice of an Arhat. One must possess the stronghold of striving in order to nurture the rivers, gathering the whole invincible Service to Hierarchy. Why is the Service called great? Because it approaches the Infinite. This is the measure by which you can think of the Three Pearls of the World.

443. If I again say that the currents are difficult, the ignorant may ask, "But when will they be different?" I will say, "Within the defile of darkness the calm of death may exist, but upon the summits are the whirlwinds of the far-off worlds." Thus, guard your health.

444. The Spatial Fire rages especially when the evidence of human imperfection manifests itself on a powerful scale. The Fire, permeating all vital cosmic manifestations, rushes impetuously to the formation of new bodies. But when there are no corresponding manifestations in the vital actions of humanity, then, certainly, destruction asserts itself both in Cosmos and in the human affirmation. As Cosmos has its center of Cosmic Fire, so humanity must realize its fiery center in the Hierarchy, which guides humanity and imbues it with the powerful leading principle. Thus, one can strive to the realization of the Highest Hierarchy of the fiery Heart.

Thus, humanity must realize all the best strivings. Only thus can one progress in evolution. Verily, only by adhering to Hierarchy can one advance. Hence, in the great time of shifting, humanity can be saved only through Hierarchy. Therefore it is so imperative to realize the greatness of the Leader as the Savior of nations. The time is austere, but great. Thus we shall construct the great future.

445. The approach is endless; so, too, are defeats. Few will discern where is victory and where defeat. One must know the relation of spiritual growth to the victory over darkness. Darkness can display the Maya of well-being, whereas Light can attest to violent commotions. Each one strives along the shortest path, but who is capable of imagining the best achievements? Only the link with Hierarchy can reveal the uniqueness of the best path. Our decision is to consider achievement as the shortest path. The dark ones consider fearlessness as a bad sign. We have determined not to avoid the steep path. For them, each ascent is an unnecessary dissipation of strength. With Us, the Ray of Light is a bridge of granulations, but they dream of a void. We understand each daring leap; for them, it is but recklessness. Thus, between the daring of wisdom and the recklessness of treason stands only the heart. It will safeguard and open the Gates of Hierarchy. He will err less who follows the silver thread stretched from his heart to the heart of the Teacher.

446. It is necessary to accept the one direction to that Heart where there is no refusal. The channel of the heart must be purified. Will it not be the protecting net of the planet, like the silver threads of desti-

nies? One should not think of the heart as a blob of lower matter. If so, how to contact the Highest World?

One must accustom oneself to the thought of victory. Otherwise, how many defeats are but the consequences of indifference. Indifference is already defeat; as in the present, so in the future.

447. During great constructions, certainly the battle is also great, because the dark ones are afraid of losing their weapons. Thus, each striving directed to the Good undoubtedly calls forth attacks. However, one should understand the invulnerability of the servitor of Light, for when the heart is flamingly imbued with the Hierarchy, all hostile attacks can be overcome. Indeed, it must be understood that each personal feeling undermines the roots of the great structure. Thus, so much of the wondrous is destroyed by humanity, because Leadership was rejected. Therefore no one will be successful who has not realized the greatness of Leadership. Thus, the closest and the most distant ones must sense the current of each affirmed law.

448. Hierarchy is cooperation. But with cooperation, the intensification of energies results in a continuous circuit of sparks, from above downward and from below upward. The dynamo producing this flaming torrent is the heart. It means that above all else, Hierarchy is the Teaching of the Heart. One should be accustomed to understanding the heart as the central motive power. One cannot understand the flame without understanding the significance of the heart. I spoke to you of many centers, but just now I especially stress the Chalice and the heart. The Chalice is the past, the heart is the future. Now, certainly, we comprehend that the ascent is accomplished only along the single silver thread! Therefore, let us be especially cautious with the predestined structure. The chemist values a rare reaction in a certain test tube, and nothing in the world will repeat this reaction if the test tube is broken. So it is with Our construction.

449. Likewise the heart should be understood as the unique natural link between the visible and invisible worlds. Many secretions bind the lowest strata of both worlds, but only the thread of the heart can lead into the Infinite. In this lies the difference between magic and the nature of the spirit. Thus, I advise, first of all, to pay attention to the heart as the source of the predestined unification of the worlds. It should not be thought that Hierarchy is only discipline; it is the advance into the Higher World.

450. The realization of the immutability of the plan directs each trend of thought to Truth. Creativeness of the spirit demands a saturated onward striving; therefore each wavering carries away a constructive approach. The fundamental quality of creativeness is the direct following of the Hierarchy. Only thus can it be affirmed that the path will lead to the highest attainments. How else can humanity contact the Spatial Fire if not through the approach to Hierarchy? Thus, the leading principle of Hierarchy fierily impels humanity to a new advance. Without this mighty progress darkness will engulf the planet.

451. If one were to expound the condition and aims of Yoga, the number of applicants would not be great. For them the renunciation of selfhood would be dreadful. When a Yogi feels the same during want or plenty; when he feels himself only a disposer of means; when he feels his destination in bringing service to the world and his holiday in communion with the Higher Forces—such a way of life, with the assumption of all the burdens of surrounding imperfections, will not be pleasant to many. Many are altogether incapable of thinking about the future, lulling themselves with the misunderstood letters of the Scriptures. We must not think too much of the earthly, yet it is not said anywhere that we should not think of the future. The thought of the future is already like gates to the Infinite. Thus, think of the future, and you may be sure that this thought will be supported by Hierarchy.

452. One should think of Us precisely as of an Inexhaustible Spring; otherwise the earthly rivers may dry up. Much has already been said by Us about the Teaching being a source of life. It should be understood that the linking of the worlds would already be a salutary conquest.

453. How easy it is to ameliorate life only by striving to a manifest victory of the spirit! Is it possible that all the discoveries of science have not broadened human thinking?

454. When you understand the foundations of Hierarchy, We shall proceed to an explanation of the centering of the spirit in the heart. In order to link the chain of the worlds it will be necessary to give special attention to the heart. Only thus shall we keep within the boundaries of a natural growth of the spirit. The abode of the spirit is in the heart. Thoughts about Hierarchy are spiritualized by the heart. Thus we shall remain as before in the essence of a true accumulation.

455. The power of Guidance imbues humanity with all strivings. Each attainment directed to progress is affirmed by the Higher Will. The guaranty is manifested only by affirmation of the correlation between the Higher Will and assimilation. Thus is revealed to humanity a direct bond between the Hierarchy and the disciple. Thus, verily, the great Might underlies the silver thread that links all the best inceptions. Truly, it can be affirmed that victory underlies the bond with the Higher Will.

456. Everyone whose consciousness can already contain the significance of Hierarchy must first of all renounce blasphemy of the spirit. Much unworthy blasphemy is uttered and thought amidst the usual work of day and night. The most dangerous poison is produced by these imperceptible treasons. Often their consequences are more dreadful than one misdeed through crass ignorance. It is not easy to break the habit of the abomination of blasphemy, for the boundary between the white and black is complicated. We call this contamination a black ulcer similar to cancer. Besides, the meaning of cancer in general is not far distant from the consequences of a spiritual abomination. Like striving to the Guide, one should develop in oneself comprehension of the Highest Hierarchy. Ponder that in concluding our notes about Hierarchy We do not conclude anything, but only open the next Gates.

457. Spirit-creativeness is the most powerful attraction of forces. Around the seed are grouped various particles which are united by one and the same fiery attraction. Each inception can exist only through this fiery attraction. Therefore the Might of Hierarchy is that great Magnet which keeps everything in concatenation and broadens all possibilities. The principle of Hierarchy underlies all vital manifestations. The principle of Hierarchy leads the entire Cosmos. Thus, spirit-creativeness imbues with fire all manifestations of space. The symbol of Great Guidance is established in Cosmos.

458. Fear generates ugliness. Nothing that proceeds from fear can have a worthy importance. It is impossible to approach Hierarchy through fear. It is not possible to understand the application of the Highest Chain before realizing the harm of fear. There are many ways to Hierarchy. But the slippery unsteadiness of fear will not endure the ascent upon the rocks, and a trembling hand will not feel the handrails which have been carefully prepared. The condition of fearlessness must be understood equally with devotion. Broad is devotion, but you remember how multicolored is fear. A man who is not even bad may be frightened, and this infection can forever deprive him of ascent. Hence, one should cure oneself of fear.

Besides psychic energy, musk is useful, because it strengthens the nervous system and kindles the protective net. Thus the strengthening of the centers of the heart and Chalice gives a necessary strength to the protective net. Heart, fiery Chalice, illumine ye the path of the ascending ones!

459. The ways of the heart, the fiery ways that lead to the ascension of the spirit, are developed by being imbued with one and the same impulse of the attraction of the Cosmic Magnet. How many different branchings the sensitive fiery heart possesses! But its source is one, and its potentiality is imbued by the sole source, Hierarchy. The ways of the heart, the fiery ways, proceed from the great summit of Hierarchy and lead to that Pearl of the World. Thus, We affirm the flame of the heart and the wondrous silver thread that unites the worlds. Thus we conquer through creativeness manifested by the silver thread.

460. A valiant eye will not be dulled. A valiant eye will look into the sun of Hierarchy. Not cringing, not irritation, not profit, will be the gates to Hierarchy. But willing Service, a heartfelt veneration, and conscious ascent will bring one to the threshold of Light.

We finish Our writing on this Great Day, when one more step of Satya Yuga has begun. The step of ascent was proclaimed through scriptures long ago, but the dust of the bazaar dulled people's eyes. So it is today. It will again be asked, "Where is the trumpet call, where are the wings of the angels, where is the sundering of mountains and seas?" The blind ones take the tempest for a call to the repast.

Thus, the cure is in the realization of the Hierarchy of the Heart. The Teaching will be revealed to those who have perceived the right path. The Messenger will knock at their door.

AGNI YOGA SERIES

Leaves of Morya's Garden I (The Call)	1924
Leaves of Morya's Garden II (Illumination)	1925
New Era Community	1926

Signs of Agni Yoga

Agni Yoga	1929
Infinity I	1930
Infinity II	1930
Hierarchy	1931
Heart	1932
Fiery World I	1933
Fiery World II	1934
Fiery World III	1935
Aum	1936
Brotherhood	1937
Supermundane (in 3 volumes)	1938

Agni Yoga Society
www.agniyoga.org

www.ingramcontent.com/pod-product-compliance
Lightning Source LLC
Chambersburg PA
CBHW061646040426
42446CB00010B/1612